1983

CENSORSHIP AND OBSCENITY

Censorship
and Obscenity

edited by RAJEEV DHAVAN
and CHRISTIE DAVIES

ROWMAN AND LITTLEFIELD
TOTOWA, NEW JERSEY

First published in the United States 1978
by Rowman and Littlefield, Totowa, N.J.

ISBN 0-8476-6054-0.

Printed in Great Britain

Contents

Acknowledgements

Some of these contributions are revised versions of papers for a conference on censorship organised jointly by Brunel University and *Forum* magazine. The conference did not take place. But, this book would be incomplete without acknowledging our debt to Molly McKellar, who got the various interested parties together with charm, tact and skill. Philip Hodson, *Forum's* editor, was one of the organisers of the conference and provided valuable assistance along with the rest of *Forum's* staff. The Student's Union at Brunel – in particular Mr. Philip Stopford – took on a large part of the administrative load. Miss Carolyn Hudson of the Law Department at Brunel provided invaluable assistance in acting as an *ex officio* secretary to the conference. We are grateful to all these people, and to Mr. Edward Elgar of Martin Robertson and to the editors of this series.

Rajeev Dhavan
Christie Davies

Preface

by John Trevelyan

The editors of this book have collected papers written by experts on those aspects of obscenity and the law in which they have direct experience and special knowledge. As will be seen the writers are mainly distinguished psychiatrists and lawyers who are able to make an important contribution to the censorship debate. These papers recognise valid arguments on both sides of the controversy and provide an unusually objective analysis of the problems in this field.

This is an area in which there are few certainties and little evidence, so far, to support either one side of the case or the other. The ultimate test is in human behaviour, about which, even now, comparatively little is known. As Masaryk once said, 'Man is a damned complicated puzzling piece of mechanism, and no two men are the same'. The relative lack of reliable evidence on this subject has long been made use of by both sides in the debate, and it is now time to consult the kind of wisdom and intelligence which, in my opinion, this book offers.

It has often been claimed, with some justification, that the British have a genius for compromise. If, through 'meaningful discourse', it proves possible to find workable and sensible solutions to the present problems we may be able to attain a state of greater enlightenment and good sense, and in doing so, be of some help to other nations. But this can only be achieved if the principal protagonists are prepared to adopt more objective attitudes than have been evident in recent years.

What is needed is open debate that is objective and rational, and not emotive. Of course as individuals, we have every right to our own opinions, and every right to express them. But we must recognise that people who have different opinions from ours have these rights too.

What we must constantly remember is that our aim and purpose should be to help individuals of all kinds as well as society. We must try to hold a fair balance between human freedom, which most people regard as being of fundamental importance, and the risk of harm, such as it may be. It is not an easy balance to determine but it is the core of the problem.

A disinterested analysis is of particular importance now for two reasons. First, it is widely recognised, by both sides in the debate, that the time is approaching, at least in Britain, when new decisions will have to be made by Parliament: existing legislation dealing with obscenity and indecency is unsatisfactory in many ways. Secondly, it has become urgent now to establish some firm and rational guidelines because of marked changes in our social structure and in personal and public attitudes. In the course of my lifetime we have moved from a world of apparent security to a world of frightening uncertainty, and from a society that was based ostensibly on Christian values to a more materialistic society in which such values are no longer universally accepted. In this country, as in many others, we have observed what has seemed to be a tidal wave of sex preoccupation together with an obsessive attraction to violence. The commercial exploitation of these developments has produced enormous profits, never greater than when the merchandise is technically illegal.

We may attribute to this, rightly or wrongly, many of the ills of our society, but we cannot ignore it, nor can we put the clock back. We must see things as they are and try to find the right way ahead. It is not just a question of what we personally like or dislike, but of what we seriously believe to be right for the people who live in the world today; and since what is decided in our time is likely to continue for some years, we must try to envisage the kind of world in which the young of today will be adult citizens. In doing this we should not ignore the experience of the past, and we should be ready to learn from the experience of other countries.

In a world which must live with the threat of nuclear destruction the extent to which society should free or control the availability of obscenity and pornography may seem to some people to be a relatively unimportant matter. But the debate is more far-reaching than that. It is concerned with the ethos of the society in which our children will live, and with their personal freedom. If, as I hope, this book will help people to think clearly about these problems, and to realise that there are no easy and certain answers, then it will have achieved its purpose.

to Shanti and Shakuntala Dhavan
Christopher Davies
and the memory of Marian Davies

Introduction

by Christie Davies

There are many books on the controversial subject of the censorship of obscenity but most of them provide only a very restricted analysis of a few themes. The author informs his readers of the current state of the law, tells them what the law ought to be and provides only such information as is relevant to the case he is making. In this work we propose to take a broader view. In addition to providing evidence relating to the question 'What should be censored', we wish to pose other questions of equal interest to the reader interested in the relationships between law, morality and society. Censorship is not just a product of the disputes of rival groups of social philosophers. The censorship of obscenity is a social fact, a reflection of a social order in which some groups impose or seek to impose a set of moral rules on others. Certain obvious questions stem from this: who are the groups who have or seek the power of censorship? How are the censorship laws interpreted and administered? What effect does the imposition of such restrictions have on the consumer or would-be consumers of pornography?

In addition to broadening the range of questions asked, we have sought also to broaden the range of evidence seen as relevant. We have brought together the work of lawyers, sociologists and psychologists who have all used their special skills to analyse a common problem. Just as our authors are not all drawn from a single field, neither is our evidence restricted to a single country or time period. As in most books written on this subject in the English language much of our concern is with the present-day situation in England and America. However, our authors do look carefully and comparatively at other countries and eras and mention is made of the legal and social situation in countries as diverse as Denmark, Scotland and India.

In posing the first question, 'Who censors obscenity?' we have concentrated our attention on the Anglo-Saxon countries and Britain in particular. Our authors look at Parliament, at pressure groups and at lawyers and judges and seek to provide descriptions of the opinions held about censorship by different groups at different times together with an analysis of the social background that moulded the formation of such opinions. Christie Davies attempts to analyse the changes in Parliamentary opinion on the question of the censorship of obscenity in terms of the 'moralist–causalist' model that he has earlier used (in his book *Permissive Britain,* Pitman, London, 1975) to explain the growth of 'permissive' legislation on divorce, abortion, capital punishment, etc. A 'moralist' in this model is one who decides whether or not an activity should be banned by law on the basis of the intrinsic wickedness (or virtue) of the activity concerned. A causalist by contrast asks the question 'Regardless of whether this activity is *per se* good or bad will more harm be done by banning it or by permitting it?' In general the causalist outlook has made for greater permissivness, but it need not necessarily do so for the causalist is as indifferent to the moralist claims of the libertarian as to those of the puritan. Davies' thesis is that Parliamentary opinion has shifted from moralism to causalism during the last thirty years as a result of the bureaucratisation of British society.

However, there still exists among the British people a substantial number of moralists and these have organised themselves into powerful pressure groups to resist the drift into permissiveness. In relation to questions of obscenity and censorship the most important moralist pressure group has been Mrs. Mary Whitehouse's National Viewers and Listeners Association, the group that set out to 'Clean up T.V.' Doctors Tracey and Morrison of the Mass Communication Research Centre at Leicester University have done an in-depth study of NVALA and interviewed many of its members. The importance of Tracey and Morrison's analysis lies in their accurate and courageous demolition of the fashionable sociological treatment of moral crusades such as NVALA. They clearly demonstrate what many of us have long suspected, that moral crusades such as NVALA are not simply or primarily an expression of anguish by a group or class that has lost economic power or social status. They show that there exists a realm of moral action in which persons making moral assertions mean exactly what they say. If Mrs. Whitehouse says she wants to clean up T.V. she means she wants to clean up T.V. and not that she wishes to protest about the eclipse of small entrepreneurs by big business. There is of course a background of on-going social change, notably the overall secularisation of society which, in turn, reflects other social changes such as bureaucratisation; and this no doubt led to the formation of NVALA. However, the links between the changes in the social structure and changes in people's moral outlook are much more indirect and diffuse than sociologists like to think.

If we bring lawyers and judges into the category of social groups determining 'who censors' we are inexorably forced to try and answer the related question 'How does censorship work?' Further, we are forced to come to grips with the question that has so far dominated the debate on censorship and obscenity, 'What should the laws of censorship seek to do?' This latter question tends to be asked in isolation but here we have placed it alongside a number of relevant empirical questions. Fact and value can and should be separated, but they can only be studied together.

One essential method of answering these questions is to do a comparative analysis of how obscenity laws operate in different legal systems and societies. Dr. Rajeev Dhavan, who has direct experience of how the legal systems operate in several countries, has looked at the experience of other democratic countries besides Britain and America. The framing and enforcing of obscenity laws in such countries is more diverse than is usually realised and Dr. Dhavan's detailed knowledge of the relevant legal machinery and practice of countries as different as New Zealand and India enables him to make some illuminating comparisons.

Broad studies like these are vital for a fuller understanding of the censorship of obscenity but they are not the only way of obtaining new knowledge or creating new theories. Equally useful are detailed analyses of particular facets of censorship such as those of Professor MacCormick and John Trevelyan. Professor MacCormick takes a problem that has recently exercised the minds of judges and lawyers in both Britain and America – the relationship between privacy and obscenity. This problem has cropped up in two very different contexts. The first is the question of whether (and under what circumstances) the possessor and consumer of obscene material should be free from unwanted intrusions into his privacy by law enforcement officials. The second question is whether flagrantly and publicly displayed obscene materials are an invasion of the privacy of the casual passer-by. Professor MacCormick brings to these difficult and important issues subtle and rigorous arguments which expose the difficulties inherent in the use of the concepts 'privacy' and 'obscenity' within a legal framework.

John Trevelyan is unique among our contributors in having professional experience of censorship. He was Secretary of the British Board of Film Censors for thirteen years. Even as a censor his experience was unique for as he points out 'film censorship is the only external censorship of the media of communication and entertainment that survives in Britain', and there is no other country that operates a similar system of film censorship. To be in charge of such a distinctive body is necessarily to be aware of differences and comparisons between one's own and other modes of censorship. John Trevelyan's historical account of the development of film censorship in Britain and of the legal and political pressures that can threaten the film maker and distributor is more than a description of one kind of censorship of one medium. It is also the basis for general moral reflections on the question of whether we need censorship at all.

Many people nowadays base their views of whether or not we need the censorship of obscenity on the question 'Does obscenity do any harm?' Indeed vast sums of money have been spent in the United States and elsewhere trying to find the answer to this question. It may well be objected that in addition to trying to measure the harm that springs from the dissemination of obscene material, we ought also to try and measure the good that it does. Dr. Gillan in her paper 'Therapeutic Uses of Obscenity' draws attention to this neglected aspect of obscene material – the benefits that many people derive from it. From her survey of recent work in sex therapy she concludes that erotica is helpful in the diagnosis or assessment of sexual disorders and contributes to the treatment of sexual deviations. It is particularly important as part of 'stimulation therapy' where it enhances sexual pleasure and helps in the treatment of impotence and frigidity. Were strict laws against obscenity introduced and rigidly enforced, presumably the sexually deprived would be unable to obtain this kind of treatment. On the other hand in a society where pornography is freely available the impotent and the frigid can attempt to use it to alleviate their condition by self-medication, much as the rest of us consume Beecham's powders or Alka-Seltzer. Such treatment may be clumsy but it could also be effective and this is presumably one benefit that flows from the absence of laws restricting the production and sale of obscene material.

A similar point is made by Dr. Berl Kutchinsky on the basis of his study of what happened in Denmark following the abolition of their laws against pornography. 'In Denmark not only was there no increase in sexual offences along with the increased availability of pornography, there was in fact a very considerable decrease . . . this decrease took place in all types of sexual offences except rape, which remained unchanged.' Some of this decrease is of course purely statistical but for certain types of serious sexual offences such as child molesting, the decrease in reported cases was a reflection of an actual decrease in the number of crimes committed. I have quoted Dr. Kutchinsky's important findings verbatim precisely because there has been so much ignorant controversy about the results of the Danish reforms. I hope that those who read Dr. Kutchinsky's article in this book will follow up the references that he gives and in particular that they will read Dr. Kutchinsky's other articles and book on this subject. Dr. Kutchinsky's work in this field has carefully and scrupulously sorted out the different reasons that could lie behind the fall in the rates of reported sex crimes. At no point has he assumed that a fall in the reported rate indicates a real fall in the incidence of a sexual crime until he has shown from other independent evidence that this is in fact the case.

The work of Dr. Gillan and Dr. Kutchinsky indicates that there may actually be some benefits to society from relaxing or abolishing the laws against obscenity. Presumably the link between their findings lies in the fact that certain kinds of sexually deprived people who cannot function adequately with an adult partner use pornography and child molestation as alternative modes of gaining sexual satisfaction. I have stressed these positive consequences of freely available obscene materials mainly because the popular debate has raged around the question of whether or not pornography is harmful. To redress the balance it is important to state that there is potential good as well as harm in the obscene materials that have so excited public controversy. However, it would provide an equally unbalanced picture to omit the fact that some psychologists see obscenity as harmful to the individual and society. It falls to our final contributor Professor H. J. Eysenck to assess the overall gains and losses that society may derive from pornography. Perhaps his most telling point is that 'pornography does not have one set of consequences but many; some might be considered good, others bad. Furthermore what is good to one person may be bad for another; individuality is supreme in this field'.

SECTION I

Who Censors and Why?

How our Rulers Argue about Censorship

by Christie Davies

During the last twenty-five years or so society has chosen to exercise less and less censorship of books, newspapers and illustrated magazines, of films, plays, radio and television. Writers and broadcasters can now freely discuss and illustrate areas of life that used to be taboo subjects and there is much greater freedom for them in their choice of language and mode of presentation. Scenes in books, plays, films or broadcasts that would in the past have been censored are now freely shown. This withering away of the censor is often analysed as part of those more general changes which have given rise to 'the permissive society'. Here, as in other areas, Parliament is seen to play a key role. The permissive parliaments that made it easier to lay a bet, to obtain a divorce or an abortion or to indulge in homosexual practices without fear of prosecution are also seen as having drastically relaxed the laws relating to censorship. For some, Parliament has considerably extended our freedom to speak, write and publish – for others, Parliament has destroyed necessary and vital safeguards against a kind of pornographic anarchy.

In practice the matter is nothing like as simple as this for Parliament has, in the years since 1950, imposed as many new forms of censorship on the writer as it has weakened or abolished existing restrictions. The first of these was the Children and Young Persons Harmful Publications Act of 1955 which

> places a general prohibition on the printing or dissemination of any book or magazine which is likely to fall into the hands of young persons and which consists of stories told in pictures, portraying the commission of crimes or violent and repulsive or horrible acts or incidents in such a way that the work as a whole would tend to corrupt a child or young person into whose hands it might fall.[1]

9

This was the Act that censored horror comics out of existence.

A similar concern with the impact of violence on children is seen in section 4(1)(a) of the Television Act of 1964 which required the Independent Television Authority to draw up a code giving guidance to programme makers

> as to the rules to be observed in regard to the showing of violence particularly when large numbers of children and young persons may be expected to be watching the programme.[2]

Further new censorship restrictions were introduced as part of the Race Relations Act of 1965, which imposed a ban on speeches or written propaganda of a racially abusive nature. It has always been an offence under the common law 'to seek to promote violence by stirring up hostility or ill will between classes of Her Majesty's subjects',[3] and the law has been reinforced by the Public Order Act of 1936, which made it an offence to use words or behaviour at a public meeting or in a public place that are 'threatening, abusive or insulting' either with the intention of creating a breach of the peace or in circumstances likely to create a breach of the peace whether or not there is an actual intention to do so'.[4] However, the Race Relations Act goes much further in some ways than these earlier restrictions on the freedom of speech in that it is not limited in its application to circumstances where violence or disorder is a likely consequence of the words used but places a total prohibition on a whole category of oral or written utterances. Material that is racially abusive or insulting is banned *per se*,[5] quite regardless of whether or not violence and disorder is likely to result from its dissemination.[6]

We can probably also add to this list the further, more recent restrictions in the field of race relations and possibly measures relating to the rehabilitation of offenders. Such measures could make it a criminal offence to publish the details of a man's past criminal record if he has been convicted of no further crimes within a stipulated number of years. Thus it can be argued that in many ways censorship is actually on the increase, especially where violence and disorder are concerned.

Even if we look at the narrower area of obscenity where clearly censorship has become less rigorous, it is by no means certain (a) that in passing the relevant act Parliament intended that there should be such a marked relaxation in standards as has taken place, (b) that the greater permissiveness that has occurred was a necessary or inevitable consequence of the legislative changes. Many members of parliament and other interested parties predicted that the Obscene Publications Act of 1959 and the Theatres Act of 1968 would in practice lead to an increase in censorship. Furthermore the 1959 Obscene Publications Act was to some extent offset by its successor, the Obscene Publications Act of 1964, which sought to close certain loopholes in the law to enable the police to prosecute purveyors of pornography more easily and successfully. Indeed the 1964 Act was 'the first time for over 100 years that any government has taken the initiative in presenting an obscene publications bill to Parliament'.[7]

The 1959 Obscene Publications Act may be represented as a package deal intended to please both the libertarians and aesthetes who wanted to free noteworthy literature from censorship and those who wished to see pornography vigorously suppressed. Indeed one member of parliament, Ronald Bell, made this explicit: 'I know that as a sort of make-weight in the Bill two – possibly three – provisions are included which, it is said, will tighten up the administration of the law so that while allowing greater freedom for literature, at least there will be greater severity in punishing pornography'.[8]

The supporters of the 1959 Act stressed that they did not intend or expect there to be a great outburst of pornography following the change in the law being discussed. Eric Fletcher M.P. declared 'I do not believe that it will do anything to increase the distribution of pornographic literature. We would all agree that there is far too much pornography in this country today; in fact it is one of the scandals of our time that much blatant pornography passes with immunity'.[9]

The 1959 Act did not, in practice succeed in strengthening 'the powers for suppressing the pornography trade'. [10] Indeed, in introducing the government's Obscene Publications Act in 1964 the Joint Under-Secretary of State, Mr. C. M. Woodhouse, declared that 'the Act has been less effective than Parliament had intended in checking the dissemination of pornography for which no literary or other merits could possibly be claimed'.[11] This view was endorsed by the veteran puritan, Sir Cyril Black:

When the 1959 legislation was before Parliament there was a general hope that it would improve the position about the publication of pornographic literature and would make it easier for the courts to deal with this evil . . . many people have been very disappointed with the consequences of the 1959 Act as these consequences seem to be entirely different from what was then expected by many people.[12]

Sir Cyril went on to deplore the fact that between 1959 and 1964 there had been a big rise in the output of obscene literature, a fall in its prices and an expansion of the size of the market. This rare outburst of improved productivity in a leading British industry did not commend itself to him. Possibly he may have been deliberately deceived by the supporters of the 1959 Act who knew full well what its results would be and had only made a pretence of wishing to suppress pornography. However, I do not think this is the real explanation. To my mind the 1959 Act was in certain respects repressive and intended to be so (as part of the bargain for freeing 'literature') but it failed to achieve this end, because of extraneous social changes which Parliament could do little to control.

The Theatres Act appears on the face of it the simple abolition of the theatre censor, the Lord Chamberlain. With the ending of this odd restriction theatre producers are now free to put on plays which previously might have been cut or banned by the Lord Chamberlain. Yet even here this outcome was by no means certain. The system of licensing plays in advance of production by the Lord Chamberlain had in practice (though not in law) protected theatre owners and managers from prosecution in the courts for obscenity, blasphemy, etc.[13] No one was willing to take action against a play which had received the approval of so dignified an official as the Lord Chamberlain. According to the then Director of Public Prosecutions, Sir Theobald Mathew, the reason was that 'if a play is passed by the Lord Chamberlain then I (the D.P.P.) cannot prosecute because, once again, I should have to put the responsible official in the dock along with the playwright and the producer . . . [since he has] aided and abetted in the commission of that particular offence'.[14] The report from the Joint Committee on Censorship of the Theatre summed up the argument of many of those who wished to retain the Lord Chamberlain on libertarian grounds thus:

> Although the abolition of all censorship may appear just and logical such abolition may in fact hurt more than it helps the cause of freedom of expression in the theatre. If compulsory censorship is abolished various forms of pre-censorship are likely to operate with greater severity. Managements will protect themselves against the risk of prosecution by submitting scripts to their legal advisers and are likely to be advised to be cautious in regard to the law. Furthermore, if censorship is removed prosecution will generally be a matter for the police. It is argued that although to leave the theatre solely to the operation of the law may in theory be right, in practice the advice given by barristers, the policy of the

police and the findings of the courts may impose more severe restraints on the theatre as a whole than if a system of voluntary pre-censorship were in operation.[15]

This point first emerged in an argument between Lord Goodman, a member of the Joint Committee on Censorship of the Theatre, and Benn Levy, the playwright, who was giving evidence.

Lord Goodman: We speak of theatrical censorship as if it were the only form of inhibition on freedom of expression, but there are many other forms of inhibition: the publisher's viewpoint, the newspaper proprietor's viewpoint. All these are inhibiting factors that weigh . . . When you come to do the addition you may find that when you have added up there is no more censorship but rather less by having the theatrical censorship! . . .[16] [If the British Board of Film Censors were abolished what would be the effect on film makers?]
Ben Levy: I entirely agree with Lord Goodman here that probably film makers would become apprehensive and we would probably see even less doubtful films than now. We cannot argue it both ways. When we are in this field of prediction we have got two bodies of opinion, one of them saying 'There is going to be an enormous explosion of licentiousness' and the other saying 'It is going to be more puritanical'. I agree with Lord Goodman it is going to be more puritanical.[17]

The Lord Chamberlain, Lord Cobbold, himself agreed with this view and speaking specifically of obscenity declared, 'My own personal view on this is that one would get probably rather less laxity in that direction if it were left to the operation of the law'.[18] At a more general level and speaking of the past he also said that 'the practical result has been that more experimental theatre has been seen in the last decade or two than would have been seen if the Lord Chamberlain's office had not been carrying out its functions under the Theatres Act'.[19]

I have quoted these disparate experts at some length in order to drive home the point that the present relatively permissive state of the theatre was not a necessary or even an intended consequence of the abolition of the Lord Chamberlain's power of censorship. Had public opinion and the myriad bureaucrats who convert diffuse public indignation into specific prosecutions willed otherwise, then a new and savage censorship could have struck the theatre. There is after all a distant precedent in the gradual clean-up of literature that occurred after the Printers' Licensing Act lapsed, in 1695, when in Leo Abse's words 'Licensed salacity was succeeded by free prudery'.[20]

An examination of the debates inside and outside Parliament regarding the changes in the law in respect of censorship soon destroys the view that is sometimes put forward of Parliament as having imposed a permissive way of life on an unwilling nation. Rather we can say that in recent years Parliament has imposed new forms of censorship on the people in ways that they probably did not want. Further, where a permissive situation has emerged as the result of a change in the law, this has been the result not of Parliament's expressed intentions but of the way in which public opinion and opinion leaders have interpreted and exploited the change. Juries have, over time, become less willing to convict authors or publishers of obscenity. Their attitude has then communicated itself to prosecutors and in particular to the relevant officials in the office of the Director Public Prosecutions. The publisher F. J. Warburg speaking of the spate of trials for obscenity that occurred in the year 1954 commented, 'had the prosecution won all or most of their cases, there were many writs issued by the Director of Public Prosecutions but that were not delivered to publishers because the early results of the campaign were not sufficiently favourable'.[21] The inaction of the prosecutors in turn created and coincided with a change in attitudes on the part of the police, the Home Office, pressure groups and local moral and religious leaders. They ceased to send obscene works to the prosecutor or to agitate for prosecution.

Finally, as the external pressures were removed authors and publishers, producers and directors ceased to censor or pre-censor themselves. Their concept of what was permissible or what they could get away with changed radically. Sometimes television, sometimes the theatre, at other times books took the lead in pressing towards a more permissive situation. As one sector advanced, so the others would use its example as an excuse for playing leapfrog. In this way the real restraints of unofficial censorship were eroded. In the past periods of prosecution have resulted in a state of affairs where 'printers have read their manuscripts with great care, read them for pornography and obscenity and clamped down their own censorship'.[22] The printers have done this because they are liable to be prosecuted along with the publisher – once again F. J. Warburg explains this well:

> the printer who has nothing to gain and everything to lose by a prosecution presents himself and says: 'You will clean this up or we will not print the book'. This is common. In view of the fact that there is a

shortage of printing facilities we cannot go round the corner to another printer and say: 'Take this book, because Mr. So-and-so is too cowardly to print it'. We cannot do that. There is, therefore, an unofficial censorship on books, particularly on novels but on books generally which is due to the printers' natural prudence . . . as he is involved in any prosecution and as it can do him a great deal of harm in his home town – he will not be asked for instance to print the prospectus for the local church bazaar in future if he is called to be present in a damaging connection at the Old Bailey – for these reasons he is very cautious.[23]

Here we see spelled out the mechanism by which censorship restrictions manifest themselves through a large number of inter-related decisions and attitudes.[24] In a situation of increasing permissiveness the whole system works in reverse. The relationship between authors, publishers and producers on the one hand and the various levels of censoring authority is a two-way one. In a period of increasing permissiveness this two-way relationship becomes an endless spiral by which increasingly permissive decisions by the 'censors' permit ever more obscene literature, which is then used as an argument for relaxing standards of censorship even further. What is just allowed to be published today becomes tomorrow's standard fare, which is then used as a base for judging what can now just be allowed to be published.

This process of piecemeal advance through mass action has been far more important in liberalising censorship in Britain in recent years than sudden organised legislative action. The gradual shift in the interpretation of the rules has been a more significant factor than any deliberate alteration of the rules in a permissive direction. This point was certainly brought home to Members of Parliament discussing how the censorship laws should be changed. Sir Patrick Spens when acting as Chairman of the Select Committee on the Obscene Publications Bill noted that 'if you lower the standard to admit the marginal book you automatically raise the probability of a fresh standard being put which will include for publications an element of pornography'.[25] In a similar vein in a memorandum to the Joint Committee on the Censorship of the Theatre, Peter Lloyd of the Conservative Bow Group pointed out how the Lord Chamberlain's position had been steadily eroded long before he was abolished: 'given a free society which will permit no moral code to be forced on it from above, he is virtually powerless to prevent the erosion of and totally incapable of promoting any permanent moral line. In fact the Lord Chamberlain has tacitly admitted that he does not really

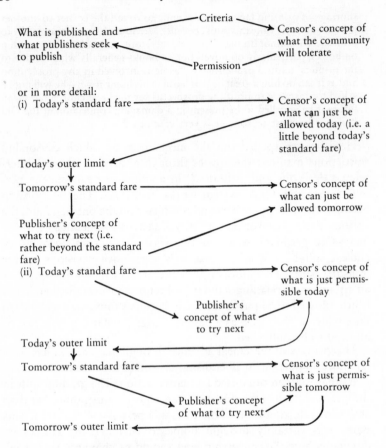

attempt to do either when he said recently 'my personal objective is to try and assess the norm of educated adult opinion and if possible to keep just ahead of it'. Despite the 'personal' it would appear that this has been the practice of other Lord Chamberlains before him. In the thirties, when the subject of homosexuality was generally taboo, references to it were not admitted on stage. In the fifties polite society decided that it was an acceptable topic for earnest discussion and the Lord Chamberlain duly lifted the ban. No hint here of preserving morals – just a determination not to offend . . . it is perfectly clear that the Lord Chamberlain is not really concerned with morals but with what he gauges to be the prejudices of the average audience.'[26]

Censorship reforms differ from the other liberal reforms in fields such as abortion, homosexuality, divorce and capital punishment, in that Parliament has not played a dominant role. The accusation is often made that a permissive Parliament forced these reforms on an unwilling or uninterested people.[27] There is some truth in this, especially as regards capital punishment. Even where there was agreement between Parliament and people that the law should be reformed, as in the case of abortion, the criteria used by the two groups to assess various detailed aspects of the reforms were completely different.[28] However, this accusation cannot be levelled at Parliament in the case of the withering away of the censor. Parliament was merely keeping in step with changes happening in society at large.

There is another important difference between the reform of the laws relating to censorship and reform on issues such as abortion or capital punishment. Over time Members of Parliament have shifted in their style of argument on these later issues from what I term 'moralism' to what I term 'causalism'.[29] In the past the decision as to whether to allow or prohibit a particular action was made on what I would term 'moralist' grounds. Those in favour of prohibiting some particular activity would argue that it was wrong or wicked in itself and that this was quite sufficient reason for imposing a ban on it. Those who wished to allow the said activity would, using the same mode of reasoning, appeal to some equally absolute value such as human freedom. Today, by contrast, the debate is conducted rather in terms of the relative consequences of prohibiting a particular activity and those of not doing so. If it is decided that more harm is caused by prohibiting an activity than by permitting it, then our Parliamentary rulers tend to permit it, even if they consider the action to be morally wrong. Conversely, activities which they do not consider wrong in themselves are liable to be forbidden by law if it is felt that widespread indulgence in them would create an intolerable nuisance. For convenience I have called this kind of moral thinking 'causalist'.

Elsewhere I have been able to show that over time the country's moral élite had abandoned the moralist position for the causalist when discussing issues such as divorce, abortion, capital punishment, but that the people had remained solidly moralist in their attitudes.[30] A careful search of the arguments in and around Parliament on the various censorship issues that have cropped up indicates that a similar shift in style has occurred in regard to censorship, but that it is a much less rapid and complete change than in other areas.

Indeed in order to find the clearest instances of such a change in the case of censorship it is necessary to take an American example. The main evidence that there has been some shift from one kind of attitude to the other in America is the sheer amount of expensive research that has been done there to try to test and measure the effects of, say, pornographic literature or television violence on the behaviour of their consumers. Only people wishing to provide answers to essentially causalist questions would finance research on such issues as 'Does television violence cause viewers to behave aggressively?' or 'Does the wider dissemination of pornography lead to more or fewer sex crimes?' Millions of dollars have been spent in several countries by the American Commission on Obscenity and Pornography and the Surgeon General's commission on the effects of television violence to try and provide answers to these questions. As a result the causalists have, for the first time, got data they can use in argument and we can expect an acceleration of the spiral.

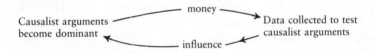

Causalist arguments become dominant — money → Data collected to test causalist arguments — influence →

The beginning of one version of the spiral in America and the change from moralist to causalist arguments there, is clearly shown in the dissenting minority report of Commissioners Morton A. Hill S. J. and Winfrey C. Link of the American Commission on Obscenity and Pornography, in their section on the history of the creation of the commission:

> For several years prior to 1976 legislation to create a Commission on Obscenity and Pornography was introduced into the Congress. It passed the Senate each time and each time died in House Committee. Legislation was vigorously opposed by the American Civil Liberties Union which reads the First Amendment in an absolutist way. Their position that 'obscenity as much as any other form of speech or press, is entitled to the protection of the First Amendment' can be found in an *amicus* brief in Jacobellis v. Ohio (1964) among others. In 1967, however, the feeling of the Congress was such that legislation to create a Commission was certain to pass. Now, the A.C.L.U. strategy changed. In April of that year, the Director of the Washington office of the American Civil Liberties Union testified on such legislation before the House sub-committee on Education

and Labor. He called for 'scientific studies' into effects on the part of such a Commission and maintained that the public and private groups should not be involved in the workings of the Commission. A bill to create the Commission was considered by the Senate in May of 1967. The bill made no mention of effects studies and drew for membership from both houses of Congress, from various governmental agencies, education, media, state attorneys general, prosecutors and law enforcement. It provided for public hearings and power of subpoena. The bill which ultimately passed the Congress called for effects studies, drew heavily from the behavioural sciences for membership and the power of subpoena had been removed.[31]

The switch in policy of the American Civil Liberties Union indicates that they realised, in 1967, that they could no longer succeed in preventing censorship by invoking 'the First Amendment in an absolute way'. They chose instead to go causalist and to call for 'scientific studies into effects'. They chose this strategy because they saw the general trend of opinion and the dominant mode of argument moving in the direction of causalism. In keeping with this they made sure that the Commission that was set up was one that 'drew heavily from the behavioural sciences' and emphasised 'effects studies' rather than one which called on politicians and local moral leaders to testify their moral feelings at public hearings.

There is here a general shift in the direction of causalism such that the general discourse among both those in favour of relaxing the laws prohibiting obscenity and pornography and those against such a change is carried on in causalist terms. The crucial question is 'What is the effect of prohibiting/permitting pornography on people's behaviour?' However, even in the Commission's report one can still find moralists of both the libertarian First Amendment school and of those in favour of severe sanctions against pornography. For this latter group pornography is wrong in itself. For such a moralist the fact that certain works give rise to feelings of anger and disgust in the breast of decent citizens or encourage impure and libidinous thoughts and feelings in the susceptible reader is sufficient reason for banning them. No manifest illegal or flagrantly anti-social behaviour need be caused by such a work. It is sufficient that the work is offensive to the reader or produces in him thoughts and feelings that others deplore. The difference in the two approaches can be seen by looking at Commissioner Charles H. Keating's minority report to the Commission:

No, the state cannot legislate virtue, cannot make moral goodness by merely enacting law but the state can and does legislate against vices which publicly jeopardize the virtue of people who might prefer to remain virtuous . . . Since 1967 the flouting of morality in the states, i.e. the forcing of immorality on the states by the United States Supreme Court has gone on unabated insofar as obscenity cases are concerned . . . The Eden Theatre is located in East Greenwich Village. This is a sleazy, disreputable part of New York. The theatre is old and dilapidated. *Oh Calcutta* plays at the Eden Theatre. *Oh Calcutta* is pure pornography – a two hour orgy principally enacted in the nude. It is not possible to verbally depict the depravity, deviation, eroticism or the utter filth of the play. Male and female players fondle each other, commit or simulate intercourse, sodomy, cunnilingus, masturbation, sadism *ad nauseam*. This abomination, at the time I write this Report, is proposed to be televised live or by video-tape across the nation via lines of American Telephone and Telegraph and various telephonic communications systems. Never in Rome, Greece or the debauched nations in history has such utter filth been projected to all parts of a nation. If there is or ever was any such thing as public decency these actions offend it. If there is or ever was a constitutional prerogative on the American people to have the exercise of police power in the interests of the public health and welfare this is it . . . Many of the shops [in America] have display cases containing artificial sexual devices – penises, vaginas, french ticklers, vibrators, etc. as well as penis-shaped candy and inflatable rubber dolls with built-in vagina, etc. Certainly ancient Sodom and Gomorrah couldn't have been as obsessed with sex as America is today. What is rotten in Denmark is already positively putrid in this country . . . It is possible for me and every reader of this opinion to bespeak decency, morality, God – indeed sanctity and purity throughout this land. This to me is a positive approach which I encourage everyone to take . . .[32]

For Commissioner Keating, pornography is wicked in itself and his disagreement with his colleagues is a moralist one. Some of the other Commissioners disagreed with the majority report on causalist grounds, i.e. whereas the majority report claimed that pornography had no ill-effects and possibly had some beneficial ones, they claim that the findings are unreliable and that pornography may well have harmful effects. In essence their criticism of their colleagues of the majority report is on questions of fact and procedure, where they see them as being mistaken. Commissioner Keating, by contrast, sees his colleagues in the majority as being not so much mistaken as wicked. He says of them and of their advocacy of a repeal of America's anti-obscenity laws:

Such presumption! Such an advocacy of moral anarchy! Such a defiance of the mandate of the Congress which created the Commission! Such a bold advocacy of a libertine philosophy! Truly it is difficult to believe that to which the majority of this Commission has given birth . . . The Commission majority report can only be described as a travesty, preordained by the bias and prejudice of its Chairman, closely followed by his staff who have long advocated relaxation of restraints for the dealers in pornography. The Report of the majority of the Commission does not reflect the will of Congress, the opinion of law enforcement officials throughout our country and worst of all flouts the underlying opinions and desires of the great mass of the American people.[33]

Keating is not alone in his moralist stance in America. The criteria of condemnation that have been popular in American courts and among American lawyers – such as 'dirt for dirt's sake, the leer of the sensualist; whether to the average person applying contemporary community standards the dominant theme of the material taken as a whole appeals to prurient interest; material having a tendency to excite lustful thoughts; a shameful or morbid interest in sex, nudity or excretion; wholly self-evidently and extremely obnoxious to the great majority' – all these are openly and directly moralist.

The Americans also like expressing moralist notions of a libertarian kind in this field, i.e. they assert that there should be no censorship, regardless of the effects of this on their country. Freedom is asserted as a moral right to be upheld whatever the consequences. The American Constitution is a moralist rather than a causalist document and is certainly interpreted in this way by the upholders of the freedom to publish anything and everything the author chooses to write and the publisher chooses to sell. As the Commission on Obscenity and Pornography put it 'We live in a free pluralistic society which places its trust in the competition of ideas in a free market place. Persuasion is a preferred technique. Coercion, repression and censorship in order to promote a given set of views are not tolerable in our society.'[34] Freedom of speech and the freedom to buy and sell in a free and open market are two fundamental liberties guaranteed to all Americans which are not to be infringed even if they were to bring the society to anarchy and dissolution. Their justification lies not in their beneficial consequences but in themselves. The A.C.L.U. and those justices on the Supreme Court who give *absolute* support to the First Amendment to the American Constitution must take up this position. On the issue of pornography they are not faced with a problem, since the causalist arguments are on their side as well: but it will be interesting to see how they respond to the causalist argument for restrictions on televised violence in the United States. Will they, in fact, retreat into a moralist posture and assert the inalienable right of the television producers to say what they want, of the television companies to sell what they please!

If one takes a general over-view of the arguments that went on in Parliament and in evidence to the relevant committees it is difficult to discern individuals whose style of argument is predominantly moralist or predominantly causalist. It is even more difficult to illustrate the change from moralism to causalism over time. The moralist–causalist model which works very well as an explanatory device on other issues is of much more limited value in describing and explaining the changing arguments about censorship. However, it is still a useful starting point because it provides a framework within which the many and varied arguments employed can be analysed. The different approaches in the case of obscenity are summed up in the diagram below:[35]

	PRO-CENSORSHIP	ANTI-CENSORSHIP
MORALISTS	Pornography is offensive to some and a cause of undesirable thoughts and feelings in others.	Censorship is a denial of the basic right to freedom of speech. Censorship can stultify literature, art, etc.
	Author's intention is a relevant consideration when judging if a work should be censored.	
CAUSALISTS	Pornography causes its readers to behave in criminal or anti-social ways.	Pornography does not cause its readers to behave in criminal or anti-social ways and indeed may cause them to cease behaving in these ways.
	Author's intention is irrelevant.	

It should be noted that both those in favour of censorship and those against it can be divided into causalists and moralists. Causalists are essentially negative utilitarians, i.e., they believe in minimising harm, misery, etc., rather than maximising happiness. The causalist does not take into account, for instance, the fact that many people actually enjoy pornography. He is only concerned with the harm it might do and the only way in which people's positive desires for obscene publications enter into his calculations is if they break the law to gratify this wish and someone suffers harmful consequences as a result. None of the moralists discuss pleasure in a positive way either, though they do not necessarily ignore it. Indeed the existence of such pleasures may in their view be a reason for instituting a ban in the first place. For the censorious moralist pornography is bad *per se*, and it is especially bad if it gives the reader pleasures of a kind that the moralist deplores.

The causalists in Britain, whether pro or anti censorship, are much less sophisticated in their arguments and their use of evidence on this issue than on others. Whereas the parliamentary debaters on capital punishment or abortion drew on detailed statistical or documentary evidence to support their views (regardless of which side they were on), the same cannot be said of the debates on the various aspects of censorship. Most of the disputants were entirely ignorant of the research evidence that was available and even those who did mention such evidence presented it half apologetically and without attempting to assess its validity. Thus in the debate on the Children (Harmful Publications) Bill, Roy Jenkins casually told the House of Commons:

> *I read the other day* an interesting survey published in New York by the staff of the Research Centre for Human Relations of New York University which went precisely into this question. It found that it was very difficult to establish any firm conclusion but it found as the beginning of a conclusion that if children read horror comics and read a lot of other things as well there was no marked effect by the horror comics. What the survey did show was that juvenile delinquency might be associated with those who read nothing but horror comics. But this might be as much due to the absence of other influences as to the positive effect of the horror comics themselves. One cannot deduce that horror comics cause trouble to the mind without knowing a great deal about the state of mind of the child or adolescent who wants to read only horror comics.[36]

Mr. Jenkins has adroitly spotted the weak link in the causalist case for banning horror comics but he is very casual – 'I read the other day' – in introducing his evidence. He clearly does not feel it will carry as much weight as, in his opinion, it should. By the time of the 1964 Obscene Publications Bill debate he is a little more confident in his approach, for causalism is now on the ascendant!

> Roy Jenkins: One is miles away from any objective evidence showing that pornography, distasteful though it may be, is a direct cause of sexual crime or even is at all closely associated with a particularly loose way of life . . . Certainly for what they are worth American sociological studies . . . show that the sorts of people to whom pornography in literature appeals

are not the people on the border-line of crime or even people living particularly licentious lives. They are on the whole people who lead quiet, sad, lonely, deprived and shy lives. This may not make pornography less distasteful but it puts it a little more in perspective than some people are inclined to do. If one could show clearly and decisively that it [pornography] had a direct causal relationship with criminal action then a somewhat rougher approach might be justified.[37]

Here Mr. Jenkins feels able to take a confidently causalist line to the extent of offering a hostage to fortune – 'if one could show . . .' – which he knows fortune will not take. True he qualifies his reference to American sociological studies with the phrase 'for what they are worth', but he is by no means alone or unreasonable in having such reservations. However, he still feels obliged to mix in with his argument conventional moralist platitudes about pornography being 'distasteful'.

One of the few members to quote such evidence in support of causalist reasoning in favour of censorship was Dr. Horace King (later The Speaker) who referred to a discussion he had had with 'Dr. Wertheim the eminent American psychiatrist whose study of the crime comic was brought about as a result of his own clinical observations in dealing with children in America who had gone astray'[38] . . . 'As a psychiatrist he has said that the increase of violence in juvenile delinquency has gone hand in hand with the sensational increase in the circulation of horror comics . . . he has said that they immunise a whole generation against pity and against the recognition of cruelty and violence'.[39]

I have quoted Jenkins and King at some length because, deficient though their arguments are, they represent the most sophisticated causalist views put forward in all the debates on censorship. If this is the calibre of the best speeches, one can see that in this field causalism is by no means firmly established. Indeed when Doctor King goes on to discuss the nature of the causal link between horror comics and delinquency one realises that he has in fact understood very little of the nature of the research that needs to be done to settle such an issue.

Dr. King: This Amendment . . . would allow as a defence to a crime comic purveyor, 'I admit Johnny stuck pins in the eyes of an animal after reading pictures which taught him how to do it. But Johnny always was perverted anyhow and I can produce dozens of children before the court – good clean healthy children who have looked at these pictures without following up their reading by such wicked acts as Johnny's. I ask the court to punish wicked Johnny and to let my clean and pure minded client continue his work of entertaining British youth with pictures which hurt only those who were originally perverted or sinful in any case.[40]

(One cannot help wondering what Dr. King would have made of that excellent play *Equus*, recently shown at the National Theatre where the hero, after a traumatic sexual failure with a stable girl – played entirely in the nude – pokes out the eyes of all the horses in the stable! Presumably he would call back the Lord Chamberlain to have it banned.)

Dr. King's somewhat crass argument is all the more surprising because it comes after a very clear exposition of the problem by Mr. MacColl:

> The problem arises because children are such incalculable creatures. It is impossible to say in advance whether or not anything is going to have an effect on them . . . All one can say in advance about the effect of a horror comic on children is that children may be more likely to commit crimes of violence if they read it than they would if they did not read it. We cannot judge the matter on the basis that one child has shown signs of corruption after reading it. We can consider only the general effect of the publication upon children.[41]

The above speeches, thin though their use of evidence is, are models of sophisticated rationality compared with the bulk of the arguments about censorship. Most of those who discussed the subject from a causalist standpoint never got beyond the level of personal anecdote or mere assertion. Perhaps a few examples will suggest the general level and tenor of the argument.

Douglas Houghton, M.P. 'I do not myself believe, if looking back on my own youth is anything to go by, and I still think it is, that the portrayal of violence, horror and cruelty have the effect that some people think it has on the minds of the young'.[42]

A. C. West, Chief Constable of Plymouth, giving evidence to the Select Committee on the Obscene Publications Bill:

> It is extremely difficult. I did several years ago have a case where a father came to see me and asked for some advice about his young son who had gone away from his home to some lodgings in the Midlands to start his career in a big factory and the young boy had undoubtedly gone the wrong way and had got into homosexual practices. I saw him and in the course of my conversation with him . . . this boy did confess to me that when he was first approached by this individual he was shown certain photographs of what happened and the man told him that there was nothing to be frightened about, that this was the sort of thing that happened, and he read certain books.[43]

Nigel Nicolson, M.P.: That must be a comparatively rare case. Would you not say that most corruption is in fact the result of example, precept and enticement?

Mr. West: I would have said so, yes, but it is very difficult to answer the question and give you an outright, straightforward answer to it . . .

Sir Charles Martin, Chief Constable of Liverpool: I would have said that when you find these books and photographs, you find them on people who are already corrupted and depraved . . .[44]

Mr. Robinson, M.P.: If I may draw an analogy with horror comics, would you say that in that case there is a far closer ascertainable link between the publication and the action . . .

Sir Charles Martin: I have not yet found any relationship between horror comics and the boy who gets into trouble. I have not found it yet. I have never found a case among children who get into trouble where a child has got into trouble through reading horror comics . . . when I was a boy . . . the penny blood was the cause of all the juvenile crime, officially at any rate. But do you think that that was ever justified as a criticism of the penny blood? . . . I do not suppose they caused me to jump over the garden wall and pinch apples. There is no relationship between the two things.[45]

And if anecdote fails there is always assertion to fall back on. Here, for instance, is the government representative in the debate on the Obscene Publications Bill, 1959, Mr. J. E. S. Simon, Joint Under-Secretary of State for the Home Department: 'I do not suppose that anyone would deny that such [pornographic] works are *inherently* liable to cause mischief.'[46]

The straightforward moralist does not need to provide even such feeble factual evidence as this. He can simply point to the revolting nature of the publication in his own personal estimation or affirm the inalienable right of the author or publisher to write and publish what they choose. In practice, however, in these causalist days, the would-be censor will tend to refer to public opinion to back up his own sense of revulsion or will postulate an undesirable effect on people's feelings or attitudes even where no adverse change in their behaviour can be discerned. The causalist censor is a behaviourist who looks for immediate changes in men's behaviour; the moralist either holds that attitudes and feelings are important in themselves or perhaps takes a rather longer term view of the effects of the material published.

The most eloquent of the moralist censors (in this context surprisingly since he was urging a liberalisation of the law prior to the 1959 Obscene Publications Act) was Sir A. P. Herbert:

I am against real pornography which I could easily tell, keeping out the stuff which is not written for art. I want art for art's sake, even with some imperfections to come in but dirt for dirt's sake to be prosecuted and thrown away. I do not think either do much harm but we have to agree with society which is against dirt for dirt's sake.[47]

And again in his supplementary memorandum to the Select Committee on the Obscene Publications Bill:

3. No writer, publisher, printer or bookseller says to himself, 'I am going to corrupt – ' or even 'I am *not* going to corrupt my readers, or customers. The thought of 'depraving and corrupting' does not occur to anyone. What happens is this: (A) The honest writer, the serious artist says to himself: I must tell my story as well as I can and communicate at every point the emotions of my characters to my readers. If there are love or sex scenes I must be sincere and truthful as well . . . (B) The obscene or as I prefer it 'pornographic' writer says to himself . . . 'I am going to make my readers randy as often as I can – and this will be the main attraction'; or if the words of foreign jurists be preferred, (I am going to promote lust – appeal to prurient interest' (United States) or 'create inordinate and lustful desires' (Scotland) . . .

. . . There are many who think that even (B) does no great harm and might well be left alone. But society, we know, thinks that there must be legislation of this kind: . . .

4. The problem then . . . is to distinguish between A and B. This will be easier I suggest if we omit all reference to 'depraving and corrupting'. (a) As I have said this conception is never in the minds of anyone concerned. (b) If the avoidance of 'corruption' is the ultimate end of such legislation it might well find a place in a preamble though not in a definition of 'obscenity'. But is it? Surely society right or wrong wishes to suppress the traffic in pornography whether the customer is already corrupted or not as it refuses drink to a drunken man? (c) Could we then not try to define obscenity or pornography by saying exactly what we mean as the Americans do? Thus perhaps 'Any such matter shall be deemed to be obscene (or pornographic) . . . if . . . its dominant purpose or effect is to incite prurient interest, to provoke lustful desires among those whom it was intended, etc.'[48]

This is a purely moralist argument of a rare kind in which the purpose of the law is to persecute pornography (bad in itself) without hindering literature (good in itself). Other moralist arguments make some attempt to discuss the harmful effect on the reader rather than society's disapproval of the pleasure he derives from 'prurient interest'. As might be expected this other form of the argument was more prominent in the debates on horror comics, though one M.P. did suggest that horror comics could lead 'to such vices as auto-eroticism'. [49] On the whole, however, it was the repulsive rather than the seductive aspect that aroused moralist ire. Thus the

Solicitor-General spoke of 'the kind of state of mind that might be induced in certain types of children by provoking a kind of morbid brooding or ghoulishness or mental ill-health'.[50] Here the moralists approached the boundaries of causalism but some among them underlined the difference between the two approaches. Mr. Kenneth Pickthorne, for example, asked: 'Am I right in thinking that the purposes of these words is that corruption must be such as is likely to tend to action or behaviour and not merely a corruption that is worsening of the soul so to speak which escapes human estimation?'[51]

On the whole, however, the moralist censors were nothing like as precise in their choice of terms and wrapped their confused arguments in metaphors and reified analogies drawn from pollution:

> There never was such a time when there was so much concern about clean air and clean food . . . we have not shown the same sort of concern about clean books; and it is perhaps relevant to point out that dirty air and dirty food can poison the bodies of men and women but dirty books poison the soul which is an infinitely more serious matter. (Sir Cyril Black.)[52]

> This Bill must be sufficiently armed to deal with mere pornography . . . just as our public health law is properly armed to deal with the discharge of untreated sewage in public and for the same reason, except that in one case we are concerned with physical health and in the other with moral and mental health.[53]

> . . . The purpose of this legislation is to give a power to destroy obscene matter before it can do harm, a power to be exercised locally and speedily, a power more akin to the removal of refuse from the streets than to the ordinary criminal procedure. (J. E. S. Simon, Joint Under Secretary of State for the Home Department.)[54]

> No responsible authority could agree that a right to such freedom [from censorship] can belong to any man. Any more than any man has the right to freedom to go around poisoning the public water supply. (Monsignor Edward Dunderdale.)[55]

> The fountainhead of our national life should not be polluted at its source. (Sir Gerald Dodson.)[56]

Interestingly enough this sense of pollution emphasised by the moralist censors manages to communicate itself even to the censored authors. The Royal Shakespeare Company's memorandum to the Joint Committee on the Censorship of the Theatre conveys this very well.

> Those unfortunate people who have to visit St. James's Palace [the Lord Chamberlain's office] to fight for what they consider to be damaging or unjustifiable excisions invariably come away from such interviews in a

state of raging frustration . . . One author leaving such an interview recently with our Literary Manager exploded as soon as he reached the street: 'I feel contaminated: I feel dirty!'.[57]

The general impression left by these arguments concerned with pollution is of a muddled shout. The moralist has seen something that repels and possibly frightens him and he is abusing it. Even where the moralist censors are more specific in their dislikes, their listing of these rapidly becomes a rant rather than a peroration. Dr. Horace King, for example, on horror comics:

> If one can sum up what we are trying to destroy, it is the glorification of violence, the educating of children in the detail of every conceivable crime, the playing on sadism, the morbid stimulation of sex, the cultivation of race hatred, the cultivation of contempt for work, the family and authority, the cultivation of the idea of the superman and a sort of incipient fascism.[58]

This speech has very little to do with horror comics and all it really tells us is what things Dr. King (on the whole quite rightly) dislikes and fears. He is not analysing, he is merely testifying.

Not all moralists of course are pro-censorship. Some are moralist libertarians who demand an absolute freedom regardless of the consequences. In his evidence to the joint committee on the censorship of the Theatre, the Roman Catholic writer, Alan Rye, K.S.G., castigated such libertarians as

> those who are concerned in the business of writing and producing plays [who uphold the thesis] that they are not responsible for the effects of their work but responsible only to their own artistic integrity and right to self expression . . . It therefore follows that a proportionately increased responsibility must fall on the public authority to try to safeguard society from the more pernicious effects of the individualistic and essentially arrogant assumption of a high proportion of sophisticated writers and producers of today that they have this right to a strictly irresponsible attitude to their work in the sense described above.[59]

However, it was not this kind of abstract moralist claim to freedom of expression that dominated the libertarian case for abolishing theatre censorship (though John Osborne did declare 'I'm still utterly opposed to censorship in any form in any art').[60] The absolutist libertarians were demanding the abolition of the Lord Chamberlain, it is true, but they made this demand even though they expected the censorship by the courts under the common law, to which they would now be exposed, to be more rigorous than that of the Lord Chamberlain. 'This', says the Arts Council memorandum 'should be a prospect reassuring to puritans. But understandably it is alarming to liberals, who realize that not only rubbish but important work that the Censor at his best might have licensed could be squeezed out if there were no Censor and, therefore, no *de facto* insurance against prosecution'.[61] Despite these fears the libertarians wanted to get rid of the Lord Chamberlain so as to place drama in the same open legal position as other forms of art and communication. Their position is well illustrated in the running battle the libertarian moralists have with causalist libertarian Lord Goodman. It epitomises the difference in outlook between the individualist artist as entrepreneur and the new men of legal bureaucratic power like Lord Goodman.

Lord Goodman (to John Osborne): You are advocating, as so many of your colleagues are, very understandably, that the censor imposes restraints on you and humiliations on you, which one understands very much and resents. What I am concerned about is how much better off you might be or would be if there was not a censorship, because this is really what we as a Committee are concerned with[62] . . . You say you are prepared to take those risks [of prosecution under the common law]. I am sure you are and I am sure you will all go to the stake for it and willingly accept a martyr's fate. I am wondering whether any good would come of it in the result[63] . . . I think we ought to encourage climates of heroism but it is rather a different objective. We are concerned with the welfare of the theatre and not with breeding heroes? . . .[64]

Benn Levy (dramatist and ex M.P.): I am still feeling rather hot under the collar after listening to Lord Goodman (and I have to plunge straight away into controversy) when he put the view that this Committee, which has been set up has got nothing to do with principles but it has only got to do with the theatre . . . Surely it is just as important for the committee to consider principle as it is to consider expediency? And to sneer at Mr. Osborne when he was merely taking a stand on generally accepted constitutional principles does not seem to be extraordinarily helpful . . . if we take away all considerations of principle what will we be talking about? What is best for the individual dramatist's pocket? Lord Lloyd put forward in much less extravagant terms the mephistophelian view that authors would benefit personally much more, perhaps, if they departed from principle altogether and accepted the protection of pre-censorship in return for submitting themselves occasionally to a tyrannical suppression . . .[65]

Lord Annan: You feel that despite Lord Goodman's awareness of the difficulties sometimes which appeals to law land in, nevertheless the principle of abolishing censorship comes before everything else and that in this sense we would be unwise to be guided by expediency.

Benn Levy: Yes. I feel that very strongly . . . what he (Lord Goodman) really wants is not liberty of the individual but a more liberal theatre . . .[66]

Lord Goodman: I do not think you can devise a censorship law that is related purely to an abstract principle . . . I would put it to you that what we are trying to do is to find a law that will work for the benefit of the theatre?

Benn Levy: I am not . . . I certainly did not say that the law was not contraceptive of novels as the censorship has been of plays . . . What I did say was that the novelist is free to chance his arm, he is free to go into court, he is free to defend himself, he is free to call witnesses and he is equal before the law of the land. He is not below the law. The dramatist cannot be salvaged by the law. He cannot even be protected by Parliament. Now this is the ridiculous situation we are struggling to get out of and it is not the situation of the novelist.

Lord Goodman: I wonder if this is not a theoretical viewpoint . . . You may find when you have added up there is no more censorship but rather less by having the theatrical censorship.

Benn Levy: But although it does not weigh with you, this is purchased at the cost of my basic civil rights.[67]

In view of the Committee's recommendation to Parliament that the Lord Chamberlain's powers of censorship be abolished one might have expected a greater measure of agreement between the committee and the dramatists giving evidence. Yet in style and priorities the writers such as Osborne and Levy do not seem to occupy the same world as the libertarian bureaucrats, Lords Goodman, Annan and Lloyd. The bureaucrats, by virtue of the habits of thought and procedure they have acquired through their work, are essentially causalists even when discussing issues within a libertarian framework. The creative writers by contrast are strong moralists. Hence the sharp clash between these two groups where one might have expected only agreement.

The other issue that gave rise to moralist appeals to liberty was the clause in the Race Relations Act of 1965 which made it an offence to 'stir up hatred against a section of the public in Great Britain distinguished by colour, race or ethnic or national origin'.[68] The opponents of the Act asked, 'Is free speech to be limited not when it is a question of public order but when what is said is distasteful or even, to use the Right Hon. Gentleman's words, outrageous?'[69] (Henry Brooke) and 'Is it a good thing that people should be debarred from saying something which perhaps they believe to be true and important, however wrongly, and which in their view it may be necessary to say in the public interest?'[70] (Ronald Bell.)

The opponents of the bill here are putting up a moralist libertarian case against what they see as a new moralist censorship law. Causalist considerations played a surprisingly small part in the debate and the evidence supplied on either side failed to rise above the level of anecdote, individual instance and rhetorical analogy.

A similar situation arose in the debate on the Public Order Act of 1963 which covered much the same ground as the debate on the Race Relations Act. Ronald Bell, for instance, declared 'I am perfectly willing to let men stand up as they do at the corner of Hyde Park and utter continuous blasphemies for quite a considerable period of time . . . I am quite sure this is a freedom which a mature society ought to allow . . . I am not on the whole in favour of punishing obscene publications unless they are inflicted on people's attention'.[71]

This point of view put forward in a race relations context by the consistently moralist libertarian Ronald Bell clearly embarrassed those who wanted to restrict freedom of speech in the interest of harmonious race relations but who accepted his general appeal for freedom of speech and his attack on the laws relating to blasphemy and obscenity. They now felt they must stress their own general moralist commitment to free speech even though they were arguing for increased restrictions. Eric Fletcher asked,

> Does the Attorney General contend or could it be contended as it might be by some that in the interest of the hallowed tradition of freedom of speech anybody who seriously believes that in the interests of our society as a whole Commonwealth immigrants should be deported is entitled to say so at public meetings? Is he entitled to go further and say that there should be a complete restriction on coloured immigration? Will the Attorney General allege that if somebody thought it was necessary to advocate complete restriction of Commonwealth immigrants even though that were found to lead to racial hatred, he should be entitled to advocate such a policy because of the cherished traditions of freedom of speech?[72]

This is a masterly piece of humbug in which the value of freedom of speech is almost enhanced by not permitting certain politically objectionable utterances to enjoy its protection. Freedom of speech would be contaminated by being extended to views with which Mr. Fletcher disagrees. There is a further piece of humbug present here, viz. that the views Mr. Fletcher wished to see banned later became *de facto* the official policy of his party and were implemented in such overtly and disgracefully racialist legislation as the Commonwealth Immigrants Act of 1968 which excluded from our shores British citizens of Asian origin resident in East Africa. As usual the Labour Party stood on its head and sacrificed principle to working-class prejudice.

In this paper I have sought to do two things. First I have tried to discredit the popular view that Parliament deliberately and rationally chose to reform the various laws relating to censorship in a liberal direction. Second to test the hypothesis that on censorship as on such other issues as abortion, divorce, capital punishment, homosexuality, Parliament has changed its dominant mode of argument from 'moralism' to 'causalism' and that this reflects the increased bureaucratisation of the institutions within which Members of Parliament operate.

On the first issue, I think it should be clear from the extensive quotations I have made for parliamentary debates and committee meetings that the changes we have experienced were neither deliberate nor rational nor liberal. In certain limited areas Parliament did liberalise the laws relating to censorship, but equally, new restrictions were introduced. The general liberalisation that has, in fact, occurred was not intended by our legislators but arose out of endogenous social changes causing unintended consequences of parliamentary reforms. Finally I think I can say that the quotations I have provided are representative of the general level of debate that took place. They are of course selected to make particular points but I did not choose them for their banality – they are neither more nor less banal than the general run of debate on these issues in and around Parliament. If our rulers appear incompetent and irrelevant, it is because they are. They are no more capable of framing sensible rational laws in the field of censorship than they are of understanding and alleviating the current economic crisis. One and a half cheers for parliamentary democracy only.

As regards my second hypothesis, viz. of a shift from moralism to causalism, the evidence suggests that such a change has occurred but that it has not been anything like as complete or decisive as on the other moral issues. The reason for this lies in the nature of the issues involved and in the problems these create for the bureaucracy. The main problem is the difficulty of defining and measuring the effects of harmful (?) publications. Because of this it is difficult to argue a clear and complete causalist case either for or against censorship. Furthermore, even if such a case could be argued the opponents of censorship would still probably raise moralist questions of freedom of speech and of literary merit. All these considerations are very difficult to quantify. Paradoxically it is the moralist case for censorship that the bureaucrat finds most easy to fit into this frame of reference and this I feel is one reason for its continued survival in a world increasingly hostile to moralist restrictions. It is easier to assess what shocks people and make a decision on that basis than to try and analyse how depravity and corruption are induced or what has literary merit and what does not. The representatives of the Customs and Excise giving evidence to the Select Committee on the Obscene Publications Bill were very reluctant to move away from the old criteria because of the uncertainty it would introduce into their work. As one of them put it: 'I do not think we as a department could undertake to discriminate between pornography and literature. I think we would rather be thought to be censors of morals than literature because I think we should have even more severe criticism if we ventured into that field'.[73] Similarly lawyers and juries found it difficult to separate out those works that shock from those that deprave and corrupt. Sometimes the two would be distinguished as when Mr. Justice Stable said that we must be careful not to extend the law to cover the publication of material which is objectionable or rude or offensive:[74] 'The charge is not that the tendency of the book is either to shock or disgust: that is not a criminal offence . . . the charge is a charge that the tendency of the book is to corrupt and deprave'.[75]

Here a clear distinction is made but not all lawyers or judges make such a distinction and even where they do, the jury is unlikely to reach a decision involving such a fine point. Indeed, one publisher, Mr. Code Holland, has suggested that 'the average British jury will not accept that it is shocked without being depraved . . . it is the measure of being shocked, really that has been the deciding factor with many juries in these cases'.[76]

The apparent liberalisation in censorship may well be the result of a growing realisation among the legal bureaucrats that there is a difference between 'works that shock' and 'works that corrupt', coupled with the knowledge that the average juryman does not make any such distinction. Thus there is a tendency not to prosecute works that are shocking but harmless because the criteria applied by the prosecutors is 'harm done' and also a tendency not to prosecute works that are harmful but familiar and non-shocking because a jury is unlikely to convict. Those publications that are prosecuted must infringe both the causalist code of the legal bureaucracy and the moralist code of the juryman.

Notes and References

1. cf. *Hansard* official reports of Parliamentary debates 5th series, House of Commons, vol. 537, cols. 1082–3.
2. *Report from the Joint Committee on Censorship of the Theatre*, HMSO (1967), p. 118.
3. cf. *Hansard*, vol. 711, col. 938.
4. Section 5 of the *Public Order Act*, 1936, and *Hansard*, vol. 711, col. 936.
5. cf. *Hansard*, vol. 711, col. 954.
6. cf. *Hansard*, vol. 711, col. 939.
7. cf. *Hansard*, vol. 695, col. 1150.
8. *Hansard*, vol. 597, col. 1039, cf. also *Report from the Select Committee on Obscene Publications*, HMSO (1958), p. iv.
9. *Hansard*, vol. 604, col. 855.
10. *Report from the Select Committee on Obscene Publications*, p. iv, para. 9.
11. *Hansard*, vol. 695, col. 1145.
12. *Hansard*, vol. 695, col. 1162.
13. cf. *Report from the Joint Committee on Censorship of the Theatre*, p. 97.
14. *Minutes of evidence taken before the Select Committee on the Obscene Publications Bill*, HMSO (1958), p. 31.
15. *Joint Committee on Censorship of the Theatre*, p. xiv, para. 34.
16. *Joint Committee on Censorship of the Theatre*, p. 28.
17. *Joint Committee on Censorship of the Theatre*, p. 30.
18. *Joint Committee on Censorship of the Theatre*, p. 40.
19. *Joint Committee on Censorship of the Theatre*, p. 35.
20. *Hansard*, vol. 695, col. 1187.
21. *Minutes of evidence taken before the Select Committee on the Obscene Publications Bill*, p. 127.
22. *Select Committee on Obscene Publications Bill*, p. 100.
23. *Select Committee on Obscene Publications Bill*, p. 118.
24. For a more detailed exposition of this point cf. Christie Davies, *Permissive Britain, Social Change in the Sixties and Seventies*, Pitmans (1975), pp. 45–8.
25. *Select Committee on Obscene Publications Bill*, p. 110.
26. *Report from Joint Committee on Censorship of the Theatre*, p. 165.
27. cf. Davies, *Permissive Britain*, pp. 13–14 and 41–4.
28. cf. Davies, *Permissive Britain*, pp. 26–7.
29. cf. Davies, *Permissive Britain*, pp. 3–15 for a more detailed account.
30. cf. Davies, *Permissive Britain*, pp. 44, 213.
31. *Report of the Commission on Obscenity and Pornography*, Bantam Books, New York (1970), pp. 460–1.
32. *Commission on Obscenity and Pornography*, pp. 583, 601, 609–10, 613, 619.
33. *Commission on Obscenity and Pornography*, p. 581.
34. *Commission on Obscenity and Pornography*, p. 580.
35. cf. also Davies, *op. cit.*, p. 28.
36. *Hansard*, vol. 537, col. 1096.
37. *Hansard*, vol. 695, col. 1173.
38. *Hansard*, vol. 539, col. 51.

39. *Hansard*, vol. 539, col. 914.
40. *Hansard*, vol. 539, col. 53.
41. *Hansard*, vol. 538, cols. 2413–4.
42. *Hansard*, vol. 465, col. 87.
43. *Minutes of evidence taken before Select Committee on the Obscene Publications Bill*, p. 138.
44. *Ibid*, p. 138.
45. *Ibid*, pp. 138–9.
46. *Hansard*, vol. 567, col. 1557.
47. *Minutes of evidence*, p. 112.
48. *Minutes of evidence*, Appendix 4.
49. *Hansard*, vol. 537, col. 1125.
50. *Hansard*, vol. 539, col. 63.
51. *Hansard*, vol. 539, cols. 68–9.
52. *Hansard*, vol. 695, col. 1164.
53. *Hansard*, vol. 567, col. 1557.
54. *Hansard*, vol. 567, col. 1560. He is quoting Professor Odgers.
55. *Joint Committee on Censorship of the Theatre*, p. 134.
56. *Hansard*, vol. 567, cols. 1493–4, quoted by Viscount Lambton.
57. *Joint Committee on Censorship of the Theatre*, p. 67.
58. *Hansard*, vol. 539, col. 915.
59. *Joint Committee on Censorship of the Theatre*, p. 134.
60. *Ibid.*, p. 17.
61. *Joint Committee on Censorship of the Theatre*, p. 141.
62. *Joint Committee on Censorship of the Theatre*, p. 23, para. 118.
63. *Ibid.*, p. 23, para. 120.
64. *Ibid.*, p. 24, para. 125.
65. *Ibid.*, pp. 25–6.
66. *Ibid.*, p. 27.
67. *Ibid.*, p. 28.
68. *Hansard*, vol. 711, col. 937.
69. *Hansard*, vol. 968.
70. *Hansard*, vol. 711, col. 984.
71. *Hansard*, vol. 680, col. 1089.
72. *Hansard*, vol. 680, cols. 1143–4.
73. *Minutes of evidence taken before the Select Committee on the Obscene Publications Bill*, p. 66, para. 511.
74. *Hansard*, vol. 567, col. 1506 (Sir Lionel Heald).
75. cf. *Minutes of evidence taken before Select Committee*, p. 29.
76. cf. *Ibid.*, p. 129, para. 890.

American Theory and British Practice: The Case of Mrs. Mary Whitehouse and the National Viewers and Listeners Association

by David E. Morrison and Michael Tracey

In both Britain and the United States attempts to propagate passionately held moral beliefs have sometimes led to organised moral campaigns and crusades. These crusades have been the subject of much research and analysis by social and political scientists. There are many theories concerning the nature, organisation, purpose, and role of pressure groups and moral campaigns but in our research into the National Viewers and Listeners' Association we were drawn initially to the theories propounded by American sociologists on the basis of their research into the temperance movement and anti-pornography campaigns. The general concern of these studies was with the origin of particular sets of beliefs and with the nature of the leap from belief to action. What gradually emerged was a proposition that with certain groups the ostensible purpose of the activity undertaken in pursuit of particular ends (whether it be to ban alcohol or pornography) is in fact encrusted with symbolic meaning, revealing responses to undercurrents of change within the very texture of the culture. In short, the protest with which we are concerned is a symbolic protest.

Pressure groups similar to N.V.A.L.A. have played a major part in the changes in the structural and moral organisation of British society that have occurred since the Second World War. Many key changes in the law have been instigated, at least in part, by a number

* We wish to acknowledge the help given in this research by a grant from the Social Science Research Council.

of groups agitating for moral reform. Groups such as, the Abortion Law Reform Association, the Howard League for Penal Reform, the Theatre Censorship Reform Committee, the Divorce Law Reform Union, the Homosexual Law Reform Society and so on, have this in common with the National Viewers and Listeners' Association – the focus of their activity is the battle within society to define the moral structure within which man shall live.

Within the 'civic cultures' of the Western world numerous channels exist to transmit ideas about policy from the people to their rulers. They include elections, political parties, individual politicians, the mass media,[2] the administrative and official advisory committees and so on. There is a broad agreement that the most significant practice of pressure groups is the contact which takes place between their members and the administrative machinery, particularly in discussion of the details of forthcoming legislation which concerns or affects the group. However, numerous groups embodying 'causes' rather than representing specific interests are more or less excluded from the machinery of government: for example, in Britain the Anti-Vivisection Society, the Lords Day Observance Society, Campaign for Nuclear Disarmament, etc. An initial definition of the subjects here would be 'excluded' promotional group'. Because the 'usual channels' are closed to such groups they are forced to employ other methods, of which the public campaign, such as the Aldermaston marches of the C.N.D. is the most familiar.

N.V.A.L.A., though it does employ the public campaign, has recently gained marginally more access to the 'usual channels' than it had previously, for example, its submissions to Sir John Eden when he was Minister of Posts and Telecommunications in September 1973), and more recently to the Annan Committee on the Future of Broadcasting in Britain. However, N.V.A.L.A.'s articulation of its purpose to the population as a whole, as for example with its Petition for Public Decency, is not simply an alternative strategy rooted in its excluded status. It derives also from the group's belief that a moral regeneration within the population as a whole is the necessary basis for meaningful progress towards the re-establishment of the Christian society.

Before elaborating on the details of our own particular findings we must first define the intellectual antecedents to our work. Our work on Mary Whitehouse and the N.V.A.L.A. has become something of a debate with the general conclusions drawn by Joseph Gusfield and Louis Zurcher in their studies of ostensibly similar movements in the United States.

AMERICAN THEORY

It is readily apparent that traditional concepts of the rational political factor dissolve when confronted with groups whose activities are in pursuit of non-economic goals.[3] Since it is not always the pursuit of material gain which is at stake, other factors, such as loss of status need to be considered. An important discussion therefore revolves around that type of group activity whose overall purpose is 'expressive' rather than 'instrumental' and whose total 'meaning' is far from clear. Both Gusfield[4] and Zurcher[5] have carried out work on pressure groups in the United States which have a great deal of apparent similarity to N.V.A.L.A., both in ideological and structural terms. The temperance and anti-pornography groups studied were essentially 'attitudinal', and 'non-instrumental' in their concerns, stemming from a general discontent within particular classes adversely affected by changing social relationships. Gusfield defines the Temperance Movement as a 'moral crusade' and as a means by which members of a status group could strive to preserve, defend or enhance the dominance and prestige of their life-style against threats from groups whose life-style was different. And it is within the context of 'symbolic politics' that one can begin to define the work and history of Mary Whitehouse. The N.V.A.L.A., too, can be viewed as a moral crusade, a group of individuals who seek to enforce existing rules, or to create new sets of rules which they then seek to enforce.

This work in the United States, particularly the Gusfield study on the American Temperance Movement, seemed to suggest during the early stages of our research into N.V.A.L.A. that protest at 'moral decay' was in effect a cry of anguish from a declining status group, i.e. from sections of the British middle class, which, in the face of the affluent society and the emergence of white-collar groups and angry and powerful trade unions, were undergoing a process of structural relocation and social decline. Resenting the way the world is treating them, such status groups are motivated to try and enhance or restore that lost status by defining the moral codes by which society will be organised and governed. Thus, for example, Gusfield discerns two important phases in the development of the American Temperance Movement. The first phase, according to Gusfield, was based on 'the reaction of the old Federalist Aristocracy to loss of political, social and religious dominance in American society'. Following political defeats in the early part of the nineteenth century, the movement represented 'an effort to re-establish control over the increasingly powerful middle classes making up the American "common man" '. The logic of their position was that if the Federalist Aristocracy could no longer control the political life of the country, it was determined to control its morals and be accorded the respect owing to moral authority. The second phase represented 'the efforts of urban native Americans to consolidate their middle-class respectability through a sharpened distinction between the native middle-class life styles and those of the immigrant and the marginal labourer or farmer'.[6]

The group's logic, if this theoretical formulation was correct, was that if they can tell other groups within society how they will live, then they cannot have declined in status or prestige as a definable and historically distinct entity. This was altogether too neat and respectable a sociological formulation to be ignored as an explanation for N.V.A.L.A. Second glances, though, can be destructive of even the most subtle and polished theory.

The key to the notion of status discontent is that particular forms of behaviour – whether it be abstinence versus indulgence in alcohol or sexual asceticism versus liberalism – not only capture the core theses of a group's life-style but also distinguish between one's own group and all others. Thus, for example, in the United States, according to Gusfield's work, the established rural, middle classes in the inter-war years, who supported and called for Prohibition, did so both because abstinence from alcohol symbolised their fervent belief in thrift and accumulation rather than consumption, and also because the consumption of alcohol was a characteristic of those urban working and lower middle class groups which seemed to be ascendant. Alcohol thus became a kind of double metaphor for the central principles around which life was organised as well as for distinctive social location. Further confirmation of the validity of this framework for explaining moral protest came from Zurcher's study of anti-pornography campaigns in the United States. He showed that their supporters tended to be middle-class, relatively rural, middle-aged, religious, non-college graduates, politically conservative, non-professional and married. Because N.V.A.L.A. seemed to have this kind of social composition and because it certainly sought to control or determine public policy (and therefore the population's behaviour) by defining the legal framework within which the mass media should function,[7] there was every reason to accept that the Gusfield–Zurcher thesis was a meaningful framework of analysis. The following pages are an account of how we sought to apply that framework to this group which interested us and how we came to reject it.

British Practice

In a sense it all began with a rather curious naivety on the part of two middle-class, middle-aged, Englishwomen. In January 1964 they set out to change the world. They were appalled by the shape of cultural change, the apparent quantum leap of British culture, from one firmly placed within a clear commitment to middle-class and notably Christian principles, to the rather rabid liberalism and secularism which seemed to ooze from the satire programmes which became so prominent on B.B.C. television in 1963.

Norah Buckland was the wife of the Rector of Longton, Staffs., had three children, and was a member of the Church of England's Mothers Union. She had given evidence to a B.M.A. committee on young children and venereal disease and had lectured to schools on 'The Way to Happiness'. Mary Whitehouse was married to a director of a West Midlands firm of coppersmiths whom she had met at an Oxford Group meeting in the early 1930s. She was a senior mistress responsible for art at Madeley Secondary school, Shropshire, and significantly was also involved in sex education within the school. The two women had spent their summer holidays in 1963 trying to do something about the 'state of television' and were astonished that not only did they have no impact on the B.B.C. but that the Corporation's Charter was renewed at the beginning of 1964 seemingly 'on the nod'. Whitehouse and Buckland were infuriated by this apparent contempt for their beliefs and concerns and set about their task of mobilising the support of the population for a moral regeneration within the media. From this stemmed the Clean-Up T.V. campaign which, in 1965, became the National Viewers and Listeners Association.

Ostensibly one could readily apply the 'American' theory to the activities of N.V.A.L.A as did the British sociologist Professor Roy Wallis:

The N.V.A.L.A. can be construed as a movement of cultural fundamentalism which seeks to reassert traditional values in the face of massive cultural change. Economic and social changes have eroded the supports for formerly dominant values borne by a class of individualistic entrepreneurs. This erosion has been more pronounced for some social categories than others. Due to their socialisation, their continuing dependency upon 'respectability' as part of the necessary conditions for maintaining a livelihood, their greater isolation or insulation, some social groups have proven resistant to new norms and values and their members are therefore mobilisable in the defence of the earlier standards of morality to which they adhere.[8]

The thesis presented by Wallis is one in which social groupings within the old middle class have witnessed an erosion of and challenge to their life-style through 'basic shifts in the economy and social structure', which provided the grounds on which the values of the traditional middle class have come to be challenged. Using Davies,[9] Wallis continues further by stating that '. . . greater affluence has led not only to the emergence of new social groups, but to the spread of values and behaviour which fundamentally deny the legitimacy of the life-style and culture of the entrepreneurial middle class'.[10]

Though we are not disputing Wallis's analysis of social change, what is disputed is the relationship between social change and membership of N.V.A.L.A. The protest is not, as Wallis suggests, a reaction which bewails the loss of a traditional culture and middle-class virtues, nor is it a response to the declining moral centrality and status anxiety of the respectable middle classes.[11] Furthermore, whilst there is, as Wallis states, 'every reason to believe that the membership is largely middle class', there are no grounds for believing that the membership of N.V.A.L.A. is made up from 'a retreating bourgeoisie' or 'from a substantial section of the respectable working class'.[12] Although class factors are obviously important in understanding N.V.A.L.A., to concentrate on its class composition as the major explanatory factor in its moral protest, *vide* Gusfield and Zurcher, is to overlook a fundamental point about the movement: *its lack of opposition to other social groups or classes within society* and the absence of any sense of social decline. While it is certainly true, on the available evidence, that the social composition of the group is almost entirely middle class, the actual 'spread' within the class is sufficiently broad to cast doubts on the view that the defining characteristic of the membership is a sense of status discontent. Given the relatively diverse structural location of the membership, it seems unlikely that there is any commonly identifiable psychological correlate such as status discontent.

The defining characteristic of N.V.A.L.A. is in fact an active commitment to the forms of Christian practice and a profound opposition to a number of loosely identified cultural and ideological positions which it sees as being the ethical suppositions of a humanist, secular society. It is particularly concerned that religious content no longer seems to prevail within a variety of cultural, political, economic and social institutions. In short, the group's aetiology lies in a reaction to and an attack on secularisation. It might, of course, be argued that N.V.A.L.A.'s is the politics of status discontent, but that they do not realise it, nor can they articulate it. That, however, we take to be the sociology of the analyst's couch and consider it, on the basis of our evidence, to be inappropriate in this instance.

Radicalism is the keynote to N.V.A.L.A.'s work. Theirs is a total disenchantment with, and critique of, the existing social world; a critique, moreover, which is rooted in deeply-held religious beliefs. The Association lumps together a number of ill-defined but deeply feared ideologies as one abhorrent whole. Thus communism, marxism, anarchism, nihilism, humanism and sociology provide what is in essence a composite metaphor for the secular world, the complex and disturbed world 'out there' which they see as more and more likely to engulf their own world of Christian truths. The point is illustrated by the following characteristic comment by one member about communism.

> I really can't see that a true communist could become a member of N.V.A.L.A. or really have the same sort of outlook as I have. I can't see a real communist as having the same sort of interests.
> Q. What if a man came as an individual and said he had a couple of children and he was very concerned about pornography?
> A. Well, if he's concerned about that I don't see that he's really thought out his position as a communist because communism requires you to be an atheist really when you think about it.
> Q. Well, you just said that N.V.A.L.A. was not necessarily Christian.
> A. No, but communism requires you to be atheistic in outlook and therefore materialistic, and for him to be concerned about his children

means that he is sort of emotionally involved and rationally he can't be emotionally involved because he's only matter and matter doesn't have emotion, so he hasn't thought his position out.

This member's perceptions of N.V.A.L.A.'s purpose was that people join because they are motivated by religious belief or because of their social conscience. There is a recognition that N.V.A.L.A. has a Christian thread to it, but there is also the recognition that even if someone was not a Christian the question of the effect of pornography is important enough to engage their concern. But communism, seen as the antithesis of Christianity, is considered to preclude the type of emotional and critical involvement necessary to belong to an organisation such as N.V.A.L.A. and to embrace the concerns which N.V.A.L.A. embraces. The feeling of this member was that while non-Christians may be concerned enough to join N.V.A.L.A. such individuals are unlikely to be heavily represented since they are unlikely to possess the special qualities of concern which Christians possess.

It is interesting and pertinent that N.V.A.L.A.'s concern is not restricted to British society; its concern with pornography, for example, is international. If one wished to argue that the basis of N.V.A.L.A.'s concern is really about the question of social status, then the following statement, typical of many members' attitudes, is difficult to interpret. During the course of the interview, reference was made to the presence of foreign speakers at N.V.A.L.A.'s Annual Convention and the interviewee was asked whether he was concerned with pornography in other countries:

> Oh yes, I view pornography with alarm wherever it is. That's independent of national boundaries. It's not just happening in England. It's of equal alarm if it's happening in Germany or anywhere. People in Germany have souls to be saved. I believe that pornography is intrinsically wrong of itself, so therefore boundaries of countries are irrelevant.

The concern is with pornography in principle and not just pornography in a certain social context. It thus becomes difficult to see how their concern could be interpreted as wishing to enhance, restore or bolster their social position in the manner suggested by Zurcher and Wallis. Not only did many members express concern about happenings in other countires, but Whitehouse has actually carried the campaign into other countries, most notably in a series of speaking tours to Europe, Australia, America, Canada and South Africa.

Social Concern as Religious Concern

If then one cannot detect the basic opposition to other social groups which is the necessary empirical basis to Wallis's theses, just what is the nature of their protest? What one can detect within N.V.A.L.A. is a pervasive commitment to religious belief, which though it is linked to a generalised structural location does not derive from the relative relocation of groups within that structure. Religious commitment is the single most important characteristic of N.V.A.L.A.'s membership. We are not, however, concerned here with the relationship between religion and social class, except to note that religious affiliation prompted membership of N.V.A.L.A. and in turn that religious affiliation was related to social class. The motivation that sustains N.V.A.L.A. and the basis of its protest lie in its *religiosity* rather than in its *classness*. In our discussion of the Gusfield–Zurcher framework we made it clear that N.V.A.L.A. does not identify any distinct structural group to which it is opposed, and those cultural or political groups to which it does object tend to be lumped together as a rather nebulous whole. In understanding N.V.A.L.A. as basically motivated by a religious commitment, such 'woolliness' on N.V.A.L.A.'s part turns out not to be a lack of analytical precision but rather a product of the nature of its concern; namely, the process by which religious content no longer prevails within a variety of cultural, political, economic and social institutions, i.e. secularisation. Since secularisation is a generalised process, its impact has not been restricted to any one institution, nor are the personalised articulations of secular belief limited to specific individuals or groups and thus N.V.A.L.A.'s critique is of a wide-ranging nature. For example, the frequent use of the term 'communist', as the embodiment of secularity, rests on its functionality as a summary statement, enclosing a variety of disparate groups and individuals, while at the same time metaphorically embodying the philosophical assumptions which N.V.A.L.A. opposes.

It was noted earlier that N.V.A.L.A., as a movement, represented a far more radical protest than those documented by either Gusfield or Zurcher, since N.V.A.L.A. stands in opposition not to a group or class but to a total social order. N.V.A.L.A.'s protest is a total radical critique of the values of the extant social order; instead of secular values, it wants Christian values. However, radical as it may be, its radicalism is both reactionary and conservative. It is reactionary in the sense that it objects to on-going social trends, and conservative in that it makes appeals to the past for support of its values. Its conservative rhetoric stems in part from its class composition but much of its conservatism derives from the dislike of a world which no longer embodies, in any meaningful sense, religious values. As a result, there is a tendency among N.V.A.L.A. members to invoke past periods, often more imagined than real, when religion and the associated structural supports were intact and dominant, and other contemporary societies which are felt to have retained the joys of Christianity, as, for example, South Africa.

Given this pervasive religious commitment, it is not too surprising to find N.V.A.L.A. members denying the empirical nature of human relationships preferring instead an analytical framework based upon religious reification. Thus matrimony is 'holy matrimony' and sex becomes more than physiological gratification, since to accept the biological imperative, to acknowledge the importance within human behaviour of gratification is to rid it of its sacred connotations. For example, Whitehouse argues that man has a potentially transcendent nature and intercourse is a means by which that transcendence is affirmed: 'The sexual intercourse which a man experiences with a woman is meant to be sacramental – to express the coming together of natural and spiritual powers and experience'. A necessary corollary of this, however, is man's potential for evil. Sexual perversion, as she understands it – which could be anything from pre- and extra-marital sex to homosexuality, oral sex and other forms of 'abnormal practices' becomes therefore part of that potential. Only if man accepts his subservience to God will he be able to control this negative potential.

This bracketing of the social world with religious categories finds articulation in areas far removed from the self-centred experience of sex. Thus, most, if not all, of contemporary social ills are interpreted as the result of a decline in religion as an organising principle of people's lives. The present economic malaise causes concern to N.V.A.L.A. members not because they personally suffer by it, but because it seems to them yet further proof of the 'ungodly' road which Britain has followed. A nation lacking the benefits of Christian guidance and ethics can hardly be expected to perform energetically or efficiently once the social cohesion offered by the Christian faith has been shattered, thereby separating man from God, man from man. Greed, rampant materialism, envy and social divisiveness flow as a natural course from the 'hubris' of humanism.

I can't say absolutely because obviously our economic state is tied up with the whole world situation, but in terms of our ability and capacity to deal with it, I would say absolutely it's tied up with the moral state. I think you only have to ask what has happened to the character of Britain since 1945 – in thirty years – a change that I think nobody in 1945 would have conceived possible, and I think that this change, this undermining of morals, this destruction of moral values, this preoccupation with self-interest, all these things are signs of moral collapse.

The situation in Britain today, compared by many members to Weimar in its seriousness and to ancient Rome in its decadence, is only capable of solution when England as a nation repents and returns to God.

If we came to repentance, then I believe God is always merciful and that if, as a nation, we came and confessed and were repentant, then I believe that God would be merciful. I think it is like a disease; when you've got chickenpox you have spots, you dab calamine lotion, you stop them itching . . . When the disease goes, the spots will go . . . I believe that it may be in God's mercy that if we had some major sort of economic upheaval then people may turn back to God. It's rather sad that it should have to be so drastic.

The death of God in the minds of the population is therefore seen to lie at the heart of the various problems which beset modern societies: 'What society has got is a non-materialistic problem and we are trying to find answers to that in materialistic terms, and you can't do that'. Any attempt by, say, sociologists and even progressive theologians to locate ideas and behaviour within a social context is regarded as not simply muddle-headed but also ideologically inspired, an attempt to discredit sacrosanct institutions. N.V.A.L.A. would say that the effort by humanists to function and solve problems within a man-made moral order can only result in the rubble of broken marriages, increasing crime, rising rates of venereal disease, industrial strikes and the whole gamut of social problems which seem to hang around the neck of the modern world.

N.V.A.L.A.'s membership tends to live on the periphery of urban centres and to structure their social life around the church. However, not all the membership is so divorced from the heart of urban, industrial culture. As far as we can tell, the central principle, whether the person is a vicar's wife in the country parsonage or, as in a few instances, a shopfloor worker in an engineering factory, is the fact of church life. This leads them to bracket most social experience within religious terms. Whatever their external commitments, theirs tends to be a privatised existence of the home and church.

It is not too surprising then to find that the ratio of women to men in the Association was three to two, and, by and large, it was the women who were the most concerned and the most active participants in the movement. This not only supports the above picture of N.V.A.L.A. which we have presented, but by the same token, undercuts a status discontent thesis. If, as we have argued, religion is the key to understanding N.V.A.L.A., it would be surprising indeed if women, as the repository of such beliefs did not form the most substantial section and backbone of the movement. (Zurcher, on the other hand, in his study of anti-pornography campaigns, noted an even distribution of the sexes). It could be argued that even within a status deprivation framework females are more likely to be members of status protest groups than men since, although objectively it is the economic position of the man within a particular family that might be declining, the subjective feelings of lack of social prestige might well be strongest in his spouse. Her social position is dependent upon the man's economic position, and as such she is more likely to be sensitive to such questions. Not being buttressed by a community of deprivation within the occupational setting, she suffers the consequences of a privatised experience at home. But, it is at least plausible that although one partner may have been more sensitive to feelings of status discontent, and thus joined N.V.A.L.A. first, the other partner would not have escaped the condition entirely, and therefore one would have expected joint membership. The fact that this is not the case, however, points away from feelings of deprivation as the locus of protest and into more fundamental questions of social change, namely a religious turnabout. To the question 'Why do you think it is that there are so many women in N.V.A.L.A. as opposed to men?', one women member replied:

> Men have perhaps to go more with what the world thinks because they are concerned, correctly or not, for their jobs, their image, and not directly with their families. Also women deal much more with the young. I think they see the damage that can be done by chance encounters more and I think we worry about it. I know this is dreadful now, one isn't supposed to be, but we are still the homemakers and we are the ones who like to keep the nest safe. I think this is why we do think more about this.

Although it is perhaps not immediately apparent, this statement expresses the nature of membership, and to a certain extent the social dimensions of the movement. For example, the recognition of 'economic distance' or lack of proximity to the world of work allowed this member, and similarly many others, to sustain a position unassailed by pressures external to their beliefs. For many, and especially women, this was made possible by their restricted movements and for others, although with greater difficulty, by psychological manoeuvre. To 'keep the nest safe' translates quite readily as 'protection from the encroachments of the external world; the secular world of secular values'.

It is a long way from Television Centre in the west of London to the soul of man, and yet change in the former is ultimately, in N.V.A.L.A.'s eyes, dependent on change in the latter. There is something of an ambivalence in N.V.A.L.A.'s position: do you wait for people to change or at the very most induce them to change, or do you force them to behave in a morally more appropriate manner? The whole question of the group's attitude towards censorship is bound up with this difficult question of individual responsibilities and moral prescription. At the formal level N.V.A.L.A. is against censorship and in favour of what it likes to call 'responsibility', though they are clearly not averse either to using the existing law to enforce their position on particular cultural forms or, when necessary, to seeking changes in that law when it is, from their point of view, ineffective. It would be nonsense to suggest, however, that there is no debate about this in the Association. At the 1975 A.G.M. there was, for example, a strongly worded motion from the Bristol branch which declared a more or less open commitment to more and harder censorship. This was defeated but the problem clearly remains. The principle they like to adopt is captured in the following observation: 'At the end, the fault is in man himself and he must be changed. We must change people so that they don't want these things . . .', 'these things' being the detritus of the permissive society. Or, as another member put it: 'There must be an inner discipline in all of us and that, if you like, is censorship'.

Where all of us have failed to display this necessary inner discipline, the group has been ready to step in and create the context within which one might more readily be self-disciplined. Nowhere has this been more the case than in broadcasting, where the group has sought to change the whole system of accountability and control. For example they have suggested, since almost the very inception of the campaign, that there be a Viewers and Listeners Council to oversee the work of broadcasters. They have sought to change the law of obscenity to bring broadcasting within its ambit. Why is it then that broadcasting, and in particular television, has provided the focus of the Association's concern and efforts, when, as we have argued, their concern ultimately is with a total social order?

N.V.A.L.A. and Broadcasting: Defying the Profane

In his work on the Association, Wallis notes:

> In modern industrial society, occupational and social differentiation give rise to a wider range of sub-cultures embodying more or less distinctive life styles, consumption and behaviour patterns. While these continuously threaten to impinge upon each other and hence provide the grounds for conflict, there is nevertheless a degree of segregation and insulation of competing sub-cultures.[13]

At the sub-cultural level there has been a fragmentation of belief such that 'no man can expect his norms and values to hold exclusive sway'.[14] The cultural texture of the industrial, urban society therefore confronted the practising Christian with a plurality of beliefs characterised by a general sense of the secular. For the practising Christian, however, there remained the sacrosanct terrain of the home as an institutional base, however isolated, within which he could define his beliefs as legitimate and dominant and within which he could transmit them to his children. The Christian family, however, necessarily exists in a relationship with other social institutions and two in particular were prominent: the school and the church. It is therefore not surprising that N.V.A.L.A.'s concern and activity has also been directed at changes in these institutions. Two key reasons for many members joining the Association have been crises in the education of their children, particularly with sex education in schools, and their opposition to theological developments within the churches, symbolised by their hostility to Robinson's *Honest to God*.[15]

The importance of a manifestly Christian home life becomes keener when those institutions which previously were part of the legitimating and supportive structure are no longer in accord with the individual's own definitions and beliefs. However, the sense of isolation is actually one means of sustaining a grip on one's commitments and beliefs and it was an isolation which did not necessarily engender too much tension or difficulty so long as it remained inviolate. Violation was, however, very much a corollary of the rise of television, since, beamed into the heart of the home, were beliefs which were held to be neither valid nor legitimate because they were ungodly. During the research for this study, one member wrote:

> I believe that television has proved in practice a disaster. Many programmes are of course of excellent quality, interesting, informative and give no grounds for offence, but the overall effect . . . is in my view on the debit side of society. I believe the intrusion of the 'box' has resulted in the gradual acceptance of standards that ten or fifteen years ago would have been unacceptable in many homes . . .

That they see their work within N.V.A.L.A. as a means of stemming the tide of the ungodly as transmitted by television is nicely put in a note we received from Mary Whitehouse. The note arrived shortly after one of our visits to the Whitehouse home during which Mary Whitehouse had read to us an extract from diaries. Broadly speaking, the point she was making was that she saw her opposition to and fight against trends within television as part of a much wider, divinely-ordained plan. Following our departure, she had clearly been concerned that we would detect an element of hubris within this, that we would feel that she was saying that she was somehow special, one of the chosen (we did not). She wrote:

> I was thinking when I woke up this morning about the piece read to you out of my diary yesterday, in which I spoke about fulfilling God's purpose in all this work. I'm afraid when I say something like that, that people might think that I look upon myself as some special kind of person. This is emphatically not so.
> I believe that each of us has a part to play in fulfilling God's plan and purpose for the world. To each one of us it is special and the world waits – often in agony – for each one to play his part.
> The point I am trying to make is this – there is nothing special about me. Neither do I believe I've been specially 'called'. I am, often very badly and always inadequately, simply trying to discover and carry out my part in God's plan. The fact that my experience, circumstances and the situation itself make my contribution a public and controversial one, makes me no more special or my particular calling more important than that of those countless people who live their lives to the best of their ability in all sorts of circumstances.
> To be put on a pedestal terrifies me! There are people who do this to me and it worries me more than all the ridicule and contempt which have come my way over the years.
> I'm terrified of the pride which would separate me from God.

Television is seen to challenge within the home those values which N.V.A.L.A. hold dear. One would therefore concur with Wallis in his general observation (while disagreeing with his precise formulation of the values) that 'N.V.A.L.A. can be seen as a protest against the challenge television presented within the homes of its members to a set of values no longer accorded universal respect in British society'.

The interesting point, however, is that radio had become a mass medium before television did, without apparently generating concern among moral reformers. The obvious explanation is the continuing impact of Reith on the moral framework within which broadcasting continued to be defined well into the 1950s. It is the transformation of Reith's B.B.C. by the structural reorganisation of broadcasting during the 1950s into the very different B.B.C. of Sir Hugh Greene which, in fact, provided the immediate historical basis for the emergence of Mary Whitehouse's National Viewers and Listeners Association. Greene's policies and career between 1960 and 1969 were to come to embody all the anxieties and concerns that the membership of N.V.A.L.A. felt about the new world of cultural change and transformed sexuality. In the Association's newspaper, the *Viewer and Listener,* Whitehouse quotes with a mixture of horror and I-told-you-so satisfaction a passage from Robert Dougal's biography: 'It may not be just coincidence that by the end of his nine and a half years in power this country was riven with doubts and anarchy was in the air'.[16] Greene always remained implacably hostile to his critics and in particular to moral reformers whom he thought were 'dangerous to the whole quality of life in this country . . . [to] freedom, tolerance, adventure'.

One can, in fact, detect historically a shift in the expressed intellectual location of senior policy-makers within broadcasting. Thus one can compare statements of principle by different B.B.C. Directors General – Reith, Haley, Greene and Curran[17] – and detect quite readily a shift from the clear exposition of broadcasting's commitment to lead in the evocation of solid Christian principles to Greene's commitment to what he described as 'basic moral values' (i.e. non-Christian) and eventually to Curran's argument that since we now live in a post-Christian era the responsibility of broadcasting is to give full voice to all the various ideas current within society. It was the translation of this emerging intent into new forms of drama, news, current affairs, light entertainment, religious and schools broadcasting, and their projection into a previously sacrosanct hearth and home that provided the challenge, that led to the action that started the Association.

In conclusion, then, it was the transmission of sectional, or more specially secular, values into the home which triggered the movement. The home had become a repository, almost the last repository, of truth and here it was being violated. It was clearly time to fight back. In the summer of 1965 the late Dr. Sturdy, who after Mrs. Whitehouse has probably been the single most influential figure in N.V.A.L.A. and who certainly had a considerable influence on her, wrote to Basil and Norah Buckland. Reviewing the first year of the movement, he brings together the various themes which we have considered in this paper. It is an appropriate way to end:

> Looking ahead, I feel this task which we took up a year ago was not meant to be a passing diversion from which we could 'get back to remaking the world'. It *is* remaking the world. I have always looked upon the television campaign as a gateway to a much bigger campaign through which we would mobilise all the forces of good in the country in a mighty uprising to overthrow the forces of evil. It so happens that television was the inspired target on which to make a concentrated attack, but as one M.P. pointed out, it is the mouthpiece of the forces of secularism, humanism, liberalism, impuritanism and communism, etc. We are in fact tackling one of the main citadels of evil in the country. Sooner or later not only will more and more of the sound forces rally with us, but the materialistic elements will increasingly hit back at us (the latest being the National Secular Society). So whether we like it or not the battle is hotting up.

NOTES AND REFERENCES

1. For a further discussion of this see: D. Morrison and M. Tracey, *Opposition to the Age: A Study of the National Viewers and Listeners Association,* University of Leicester, Centre for Mass Communication Research, 1976.
2. Thus, for example, H. Hopkins, *The New Look: A Social History of the Forties and Fifties in Britain,* London, Secker and Warburg (1963), argues that the discussion of questions of morality on television in the 1950s was partly responsible for generating the legislative debates on morality.
3. See M. Olsen, *The Logic of Collective Action,* Cambridge, Massachusetts, Harvard University Press (1968); and R. E. Dowse and J. Hughes, *Political Sociology,* London, Wiley (1972).
4. J. R. Gusfield, *Symbolic Crusade: Status Politics and the American Temperance Movement,* Urbana, University of Illinois Press (1972).
5. L. A. Zurcher *et al.,* 'The Anti-Pornography Campaign: A Symbolic Crusade', *Social Problems,* 19, (1971).
6. Gusfield, (1972), *op. cit.,* pp. 36–7.
7. Thus, for example, their efforts to make the obscenity laws more stringent and applicable to broadcasting and the cinema, and also their use of the existing law in

various instances, e.g. the trial of the *Little Red Schoolbook* and the film *Blow-Out.*

8. R. Wallis, 'Moral Indignation and the Media: An Analysis of N.V.A.L.A.', *Sociology,* vol. 10, No. 2, May (1976), pp. 292–3. More recently Wallis seems to have abandoned this position and moved to one broadly in agreement with our own.

9. C. Davies, *Permissive Britain,* London, Pitman (1975).

10. Wallis, (1976), *op. cit.,* pp. 284–5.

11. Wallis, *ibid.* pp. 284–5.

12. Wallis, *ibid.,* p. 185.

13, Wallis, *ibid.,* p. 186.

14. Wallis, *ibid.,* p. 186.

15. J. Robinson, *Honest to God,* London, S.C.M., (1963).

16. R. Dougal, *In and Out of the Box,* London, Fontana, (1975), p. 238. Quoted in: *Viewer and Listener,* (1974), vol. 10, No. 2.

17. J. Reith, *The Reith Diaries,* ed. C. Stuart, London, Collins (1975).
W. Haley, *Moral Values in Broadcasting.* Address to the British Council of Churches (1948).
H. Greene, 'The Conscience of the Programme Director'. Address to the International Catholic Association for Radio and Television.
C. Curran, 'Broadcasting and Society'. Lecture in Edinburgh.

SECTION II

How do Censorship Laws Work?

Existing and Alternative Models of Obscenity Law Enforcement

by Rajeev Dhavan

It is not possible to describe the theory and practice of existing obscenity laws or to design alternative models unless one has a clear idea of the objects they seek to achieve. Some fundamental questions about the nature of the interests we want to protect or to dislodge have first to be answered. Moreover, it is not enough merely to know what interests we want to protect; it is also necessary to know why we wish to protect them. And it is important to design a model which does not belong to 'cloud cuckoo land' but which is capable of practical application and enforcement. It would be scandalous if it was discovered that a statute designed to operate against porn pushers came to be used in such a way it was 'a thorn in the sides of reputable publishers'.[1] Equally, it would not be salutary if legislation originally designed to contain, or control obscenity in matters of sex was expanded to cover the alleged 'obscenity' in propagating drug taking or violence.[2] Lastly, at least one person in the United Kingdom asked the Courts to interfere because he was quite convinced that the laws relating to obscenity were not being properly enforced.[3] Existing and alternative models of obscenity law enforcement can be judged around these three parameters: 'interests to be affected', 'goal function of the legislation' and 'feasibility of practical application'.

PROTECTION, DIRECT AND INDIRECT

In the obscenity law debate the theme of protection is of paramount importance. It is claimed that obscenity legislation is necessary for the protection of the people. This claim is chiefly based on the general argument that 'permissiveness' *per se* produces an attitude of moral laxity which is bound to affect attitudes of responsibility,[4] and on the related idea that obscenity panders to the sexual instinct, which, in turn, results in an increase in sex crimes.[5] Both these so-called 'effects' have been questioned.[6] Some psychologists have argued that the 'pandering' effect is much exaggerated, and a distinguished criminologist has shown that a relaxation of the obscenity laws in Denmark has not led to an increase of sexual crimes in that country.[7] On the contrary he reports a decline in crimes relating to sex.[8]

Both these arguments (the 'retention of certain standards' argument and the 'increase in sex crimes' argument) assume that an individual needs something more than his own individual discretion to protect himself. This assumption may militate against libertarian arguments which show more faith in individual will.

A more liberal statement of the protection argument would be: while people do know how to protect themselves, they might be confused and misled if they are attracted or seduced to 'obscene' articles and practices by indiscriminate advertising. Here, the force of obscenity legislation is not directed against the creation or production of obscene articles. It is directed against the porn pushers or, alternatively, against the indiscriminate use of advertising. It is important to note the difference in the two lines of argument. The direct protection argument assumes that individuals need protection from seductive advertisements as well as obscene items. The alternative, indirect protection 'commercial/advertisement' argument directs its attention only against forms of seduction like indiscriminate advertisements and against those who secure commercial gain through such advertisements – not against the obscene articles themselves.

Another aspect of the protection argument concerns children.[9] The direct protection argument may be that all people need protection and this does not exclude children. The indirect libertarian argument may include children on the basis that they are not sufficiently mature to protect themselves.[10]

Then, there is the literary protection argument.[11] The basis of this argument is not that society needs protection but that literary standards need to be protected. The direct protection argument simply states that if individual taste is degraded by obscenity, literary standards will fall. The libertarian's argument is more complex. If he reposes faith in the individual, he cannot readily argue that the same individual may let him down in his selection of reading or visual material. His argument may, therefore, take the form that commercial exploitation of a certain theme may result in people being misled.

A further argument might aptly be called the town planning argument.[12] It states that quite apart from the moral and literary protection of people, cities do not 'look nice' if there are posters displaying nudity on the walls and naked women depicted in the shop windows.

Recently, there was a judgment in the Chancery Division of the High Court which suggests yet another argument which we could call the individual interests argument. It found that where the posthumous publication of a father's book would adversely affect the interests of a fourteen year old girl, the Court would have the power to prohibit the publication.[13] When certain people are in need of protection which is not given by the general laws relating to defamation,[14] the court would have additional power to protect young persons under the wardship of the court from obscene publications. It is conceivable that this decision, though limited to the issue of wards of court, could be used, at least theoretically, for the purpose of evolving an individual protection argument in cases where the laws of defamation are inadequate. But before we endorse this decision with glee, we must note that the decision was reversed by the Court of Appeal in December 1974.[15] All the same, it would be in line with the indirect protection standpoint, that, rather than impose general bans in the interest of society, it might be advisable to impose more specialised bans prohibiting either special kinds of practices or, alternatively, to protect specified persons or classes of persons from certain specified items.

The Democracy–Elitism Controversy

We move on to consider what might be called the democracy–elitism controversy. At one end of the scale there is the argument that people must be left free to decide whatever they should read. Conversely it is argued that most obscenity legislation suggests that the obscene articles are indecent or outrage public decency or deprave and corrupt human beings. This presupposes a generally accepted standard and suggests that obscene articles go beyond an acceptable level of deviation from the norm. The problem then, is how to identify this norm. One way to do this is to assume a hypothetical standard which may or may not correspond to what society really feels, but which is a convenient construction on which to found the difficult task of decision-making. This convenient construct may have a dual basis of two norms, a 'Clapham Omnibus' norm and a separate and contrasted 'elitist artistic' norm. This is what has happened in the United Kingdom.[16] Alternatively the two norms may be fused – a single system. This is the method followed in America and it has the advantage of crediting the 'masses' (I use this phrase with unqualified reluctance) with artistic sensitivity.[17] Again, various kinds of obscenity may be defined into unrelated categories which may or may not be part of a continuum depending on how different persons look at it and different situations demand it. This approach is followed in New Zealand.[18]

Many people may argue that hypothetical constructs of social norms introduce a sense of unreality into the deliberations. It is further argued that some effort must be made to discover empirically how society actually thinks. One way to do this has been demonstrated in the interpretation given to the Cinematograph Acts in England.[19] The approach followed here is to let the local representatives of the people decide for themselves what films they regard as unfit to be exhibited. In this they can be guided by classifications that are given by an unofficial body called a Board of Film Censors. Another approach is that afforded by a recent decision from the United States of America. Here, the suggestion that emerges seems to be this: the Court should itself conduct an inquiry into the kind of community standards that exist.[20] The Court resolved a pending controversy by asserting that the standards that should be taken into account were not the (somewhat sophisticated) national standards but rather the (more realistic) local community standards.[21]

A Criminal Law Model

It should be noted that since the protection argument is merely based on a *pro bono publico* stand, it raises only criminal law issues. It is important first to clearly identify the kind of standards that have to be protected or advanced, then to decide how to arrive at these standards, and finally how to enforce the laws. Thus the law model required by the protection argument is a criminal law model.[22]

LIBERTARIANISM

Many would argue that the whole basis of the protection argument is wrong and that it is important to work out an alternative approach to the problem. The first argument in this line of reasoning attacks the idea that there are certain consensus standards which must be protected. Many sociologists have questioned the consensus view of society and of man. They have argued that behind this facade of consensus (the necessity of maintaining the facade not being denied) there is usually a tremendous conflict of opinion, attitudes and life-styles in society.[23] It is, therefore, argued that any criminal law system which is designed to enforce such a consensus must be based on unsound assumptions. Closer examination may reveal that this conflict argument does not by itself destroy the credibility of the protection argument and the criminal law model based on it. It could easily be argued that, although the assumed consensus may be spurious, at the same time there has to be an attempt by those in power to make this assumption in order to achieve some kind of working formula around which rules could be built. Thus, it would be said that consensus assumptions are in fact necessary fictions, and that any empirical sociological inquiry into the basis of the protection argument would not, in fact, question its validity as a concept useful to those in power.

Another line of argument taken by the libertarians places emphasis on the idea that each man is a free individual and that, after he has achieved maturity, the development of his personality should be in his own hands. This argument can be broken into various strands. Thus it may be argued that man has the general right of free volition and that to restrict this in any way is to contain his creativity. This could be further looked at from two points of view. Liberals would argue in favour of a competitive system and therefore refuse to favour any policy of restriction. Leftist thinkers might argue that creativity without restrictions is only possible when certain social and economic considerations are satisfied. Assuming that we are taking this argument in the extreme liberal form, the legal implications (or the assumption) would be that there should be no control or obscenity laws at all, except (as we have already argued) in relation to children. Such a position would take an inimical attitude to even the 'planning' argument referred to earlier. Milder forms of this argument may accept a planning restriction on aesthetic grounds.

A further libertarian argument might be based on privacy. Here, we are looking at the position of the consumer and not the creator. Thus, even if full and free conditions for individual creativity were not to be permitted on the grounds that society's interests may be affected, there should be a zone of privacy that should protect an individual so that he is at least entitled to read and see what he likes.[24] This argument was formulated in the American Supreme Court in the famous case of *Stanley* v. *Georgia* in 1969.[25] The moot question is: how far does this zone of privacy extend? It was clear that soon after *Stanley* the American Supreme Court seems to have interpreted this privacy dimension in such a way that it is limited to material seen and read at home. Thus, when a person argued that his suitcase was private and immune from a customs' search, the Supreme Court replied that this was not the case.[26] This was perhaps in order, apart from the fact that it created the paradox that a person could read whatever he liked at home but had no right to import or bring materials into his home. Reading was permitted; transport was not.

A more serious pronouncement on privacy came in the *Paris Adult Theatre Case* in 1973,[27] where it was argued that the privacy argument should also extend to private (and as an extension of the argument, public) shows, whether at clubs or otherwise. If this argument were taken to its logical conclusion it would resemble the 'indirect protection' commercial/advertising argument that we have talked about earlier. Thus it would be argued that anyone is allowed to read or write whatever they like as long as they are not solicited by overt or insidious acts of seduction to do so. This itself would pose paradoxical problems because if no form of advertisement was permitted, a person could not express an interest in what he does not know to exist. But the 'no advertisement' stand might be taken as too extreme a stand. Thus, a reasonable formulation of the argument could be worked out on the basis that private shows should be permitted as long as there is no overt act of soliciting and no gross advertising. The American Supreme Court rejected this view. They restricted privacy to the house and refused to admit that there was a 'zone of privacy' which protected the individual wherever he went.[28]

A Bill of Rights Model

Both these forms of the libertarian model ('no restriction as long as it does not affect someone else's similar rights' and 'the privacy argument') can be introduced into the law in two different ways. It could be done as a result of statute law. Thus, no statute would be passed which would intrude upon freedom, creativity or privacy. This might create practical problems because it might be found that Parliament may itself err and, either purposely or inadvertently, pass a law affecting freedom of expression. Thus, in order to create a real layer of protection, the only way to protect freedom of expression, creativity, or privacy would be by the enactment of an entrenched Bill of Rights.[29] Here, a Bill of Rights may either guarantee freedom of expression absolutely as in the United States of America,[30] or it may contain clauses permitting restrictions as it does in the case of the Indian Constitution.[31] However, even a Bill of Rights may fail to provide sufficient protection as we shall see later.

A Practical Problem

If we reject the libertarian position and accept that obscenity laws are both inevitable and necessary, we shall encounter practical problems. The difficulty is this: can some method be devised whereby publishers and artists can know in advance whether their items will be graded as obscene or not? The interpretation of obscenity laws is subject to considerable change: often the decision rests in the hands of 'democratic' bodies like local councils;[32] sometimes it rests in the hands of a jury and more often than not in the hands of a judge.[33] In the sixties in England, the definition of obscenity changed to such an extent that obscenity legislation was interpreted to cover not just sex but also violence,[34] and the propagation of drug taking.[35]

Several methods of dealing with this problem have been evolved. One way to do it is to create an unofficial board which will classify the various items.[36] The purpose of this classification would not be to prejudge the item under scrutiny but merely to give a note of warning to the creator of the item or its producer that the item does not stand up to existing tests. These classifications would not in any way prejudice either the right of the prosecutor to prosecute a classified item or the right of the judge to find such an item obscene. This sort of approach has emerged through the working of the British Board of Film Censors. But it will be noted that the certificate of the Board does not afford immunity to the film. Local councils in Belfast, for example, were happy to find the film *Last Tango in Paris* unsuitable for screening, even though citizens of that all-too-violent town were permitted to see violent films like *Straw Dogs* and *The Godfather*,[37] Again, *Last Tango* was actually prosecuted under the Obscene Publications Act, 1959. The reason why the prosecution failed had nothing to do with the certificate of the Censor Board and had much more to do with the fact that the showing of a film in a public theatre was not really a publication within the meaning of the Act.[38]

The unofficial board certificate technique does not extend to books, and even were this to be rectified, the Arts Council in their Report of 1969 have refused to assume a similar role in relation to literary works and artistic objects.[39] There still remains the insurmountable problem that the authorities might not be impressed by the unofficial certificate. In order to get past this problem the government of New Zealand devised an Official Board, whose classifications were to have effect in litigation. This scheme seems to have worked well between 1964 and 1970. More recently the Board's classifications have come in for criticism on the ground that they have been politically influenced.[40]

One way to avoid such a charge might be to give a court the power to make a declaratory ruling on an allegedly obscene item. Such a ruling would be conclusive in a civil case but would be of only persuasive value in a criminal case. This is the model that was used in Massachusetts and is becoming popular in other American states as well.[41]

All these models, which attempt to clarify the situation for the greater security of artists, writers and publishers, suffer from one weakness: they are all based on a concept of pre-publication censorship, an idea repugnant to any libertarian with his beliefs in a liberal democracy based on freedom of speech.

Ultimately, a simpler though less effective solution may lie in a consistent line of precedent which will give to artists, writers and publishers alike a clear idea of the basis of future judicial decisions when they are indicted for obscenity or under any cognate laws. Admittedly the obscene nature of an item may ultimately depend on factual estimates which will vary from case to case; nevertheless some notion of predictability will be preserved. And in order to achieve this it is important firstly that the more mechanical form of interpretation should give way to a system of interpretation which looks at the goal function of legislation. The New Zealand statute, which defined obscenity in classifications that cover five different kinds of goal functions is a good example of such a system.[42]

Before we go any further it is necessary to sum up the various arguments that have been put forward as relevant considerations for the enforcement of obscenity laws.

A. *Consensus, Morality and a Criminal Law Model*

The first consideration is that it may be necessary to protect society by enforcing a consensus morality. The only way to do this is through the criminal law. The criminal law in this particular case may have the following functions:

1. It may seek to uphold a certain kind of consensus morality in order to
   (a) either uphold certain standards; or
   (b) prevent people from depraving and corrupting themselves.
2. It may seek not to ban obscene items but simply to prevent people from commercially exploiting obscene items.
3. It may seek merely to prevent overt advertisement of obscene items rather than the 'enjoyment' of allegedly obscene items.

B. *Democratic Considerations and the Discovery of Consensus*

It may be argued that there is no consensus in a society. This argument can be attacked on the ground either that there is consensus or that it is necessary for those that rule to assume that there is a consensus. Assuming that a consensus exists, the following are the various ways to discover it:

1. By creating a hypothetical construct which may or may not correspond with a real consensus;
2. By leaving it to some democratically elected body to determine what the consensus morality is;
3. By leaving it to the judicial process to determine empirically what the consensus morality is.

C. *Libertarian Consideration using an Entrenched Bill of Rights*

This is designed to protect:

1. The right of all individuals to express themselves as long as such expression does not interfere with the similar rights of

others.
2. The right of privacy of those who wish to read or see any particular kind of material.

D. *Artistic, Literary and Aesthetic Considerations*
These considerations are designed either to protect:

1. Esoteric, national or international standards; or
2. Local community standards;

either as a part of the process of defining obscenity (as in the United States of America) or as a general exception to the existing criminal legislation pertaining to obscenity laws (as in England).

E. *Considerations Pertaining to Certainty and Predictability*
This could be achieved in the following ways:

1. Entrusting the task of discrimination between obscene and non-obscene to an unofficial body like the British Film Censor Board. The classifications of the Board are not intended to carry weight in any legal proceeding but may carry institutional weight with the various authorities as time goes on;
2. Entrusting the task of classification (as in E1 above) to an Official Board, as in New Zealand. The classifications made by the Board are intended to carry weight in a legal proceeding;
3. Entrusting the task of determining whether the item is obscene or not to a court which could make a declaratory judgment intended to carry weight in future legal proceedings;
4. Ensuring that law courts acquire a 'neutral' pattern of interpretation so that the use of legal terminology in this area is used consistently and in consonance with its goal function.

OBSCENITY LAWS IN ACTION

So far we have considered three kinds of obscenity law model. The first is the criminal model based on considerations of the protection argument. The second is a Bill of Rights model based on libertarian notions. Thirdly, there are pre-publication warning models of the kind that exist in England in relation to films and in New Zealand and Massachusetts in relation to other kinds of publications. In addition to this we have considered whether the various models should be accompanied by a democratic process of decision-making or governed by elitist notions of morality and art.

(a) *Criminal Law Models*

The methods used for enforcing obscenity laws in England are based on criminal law models. At present it is conveniently assumed by English courts that an article which is found to be obscene must of necessity also deprave and corrupt the people who read it.[43] There is no way in which this assumption can be challenged, though expert evidence can be given with respect to obscene items. The relevant section is Section 4 of the *Obscene Publications Act,* 1959 which reads as follows:

> (1) A person shall not be convicted of an offence against Section Two of this Act, and an order for forfeiture shall not be made under the foregoing Section, if it is proved that publication of the article in question is justified as being for the public good on the ground that it is in the interests of science, literature, art or learning or of other objects of general concern.
>
> (2) It is hereby declared that the opinion of experts as to the literary, artistic, scientific merits of an article may be admitted in any proceedings under the Act either to establish or negative the said ground.

English courts have come to the conclusion that expert evidence can only be given as to the literary, artistic and scientific merit of the articles and not with respect of their effect. This means that no expert evidence can be tendered to show that an article found to be obscene does not, *in effect,* deprave and corrupt the people affected by it. In 1968 a small concession was made and it was conceded that such expert evidence may be given with respect to the effect of obscene articles on children.[44] But in the famous *Oz* case of 1971 the Court made clear that the impact of the 1968 case was limited to evidence affecting children. This was in spite of the fact that the Court paid tribute to Dr. Hayward's testimony in the Court below on the aversion therapy effect of obscene items.[45] The court has recently reinforced this position.[46] For the future it is important that the 'deprave and corrupt' formula be given a more realistic psychological and sociological dimension and the question as to whether the effect of an article is actually to deprave and corrupt must be examined by courts as a question of fact and empirically proved.

The second important problem pertaining to the use of criminal law is the multiplicity and variety of statutes that have been used to enforce the rules relating to obscenity prevention.[47] In addition to statutes since 1961, the common law has been revived to prohibit the publication of certain items on the ground that they amount to a conspiracy to corrupt public morals or a conspiracy to outrage public decency.[48]

Hopefully, these vast powers will be systematised and put in some kind of order. If this is not done, all kinds of disparities will exist. For example it has been discovered that the concept of 'indecency' under the Post Office Act is wider than the concept of 'deprave and corrupt' under the Obscene Publications Act.[49] An attempt at systematisation has been made by the Theatres Act of 1968 which does away with the old system peculiar to theatres and replaced it with a new system based on considerations similar to, though not identical with those under the Obscene Publications Acts.[50] But this is not enough. Prosecutors who cannot prove an article obscene under one law should not have the option of finding prosecuting refuge in another easier law.

At present the various arts in Britain are controlled by different methods. Thus, literature falls under the Obscene Publications Acts; theatre falls under the Theatre Acts; films are not controlled by courts at all but left to the whims of local councils under the Cinematograph Acts; television is left to the vagaries of commercial companies to the extent to which they have been endowed with the responsibility of enforcing public policy. In modern times the mass media are growing more and more powerful. *It is of the utmost importance that there should be a systematic policy of research and legislation to consider their impact.*

One word of caution must be added. The request for systematisation does not mean there should be a monolithic definition of obscenity which should be used for all occasions and for each purpose. It is merely suggested that there should be a carefully thought out and consistent approach. A graded definition of obscenity or indecency is thus not excluded. One method is to provide a variable definition of obscenity with a defined range and spectrum as in the New Zealand legislation.

Section 10 of the *New Zealand Indecent Publications Act, 1963* distinguishes the following kinds of obscene material:

(a) indecent
(b) not indecent

(c) indecent in the hands of persons of a specified age
(d) indecent unless its exhibition is restricted to specified persons or classes of persons
(e) indecent unless used for a particular purpose

There is no reason why such a policy should not be followed generally.

The third, important, relevant factor under the criminal law model concerns the goal function of the legislation. If it is found that the purpose of obscenity legislation is not to prevent people from reading obscene material, but merely to ensure that commercial exploitation and advertisements do not seduce people to material they do not wish to read, then the legislation should state this clearly and simply. This has been the effect of legislation in Denmark and it seems to have worked quite well. Again, legislation designed to contain sex should not be extended to other matters.

While considering the criminal law model it is therefore necessary to concentrate on three things. The first is that since the legislation seeks to enforce a morality and prevent bad effects, the legislation should be designed in such a way that courts have the power to empirically examine (possibly with the help of experts) what the exact psychological and sociological impact of the legislation is going to be. Secondly, the various obscenity enforcement laws should be systematised. Thirdly, it is important that the legislation be exactly worded so that legislation designed to prevent the indiscriminate advertising of sex should not be used for other purposes.

(b) *A Bill of Rights Approach*

The best example of the Bill of Rights model is in America. Here, the constitutional text itself poses problems. The First Amendment reads as follows:

American Constitution: First Amendment
Congress shall make no law respecting an establishment of religion, or prohibiting the free exercise thereof; or abridging the freedom of speech, or of the press; or the right of the people peaceably to assemble, and to petition the Government for a redress of grievances.

It will be noted that the terms of the First Amendment are quite wide – so wide that 'free speech' admits of no restriction whatsoever.[51]

The real story in American courts begins in 1957 when it was decided in *Roth*'s case that although it was necessary to protect free speech, anything found to be obscene did not fall within the category of free speech.[52] This meant that anything found to be obscene did not have the protection of the First Amendment because it was not an exercise of free speech. Thus, all that the court had to do was to discover whether the article in question was obscene or not. If it was found that the article in question was obscene the constitution could not save it. This was an extreme position. It could have resulted in an extremely heavy clamp-down against items alleged to be obscene.

But during the sixties it was found that there were three trends that were responsible for softening the initial impact of the *Roth* decision. The *first* trend was that in discovering whether the items were obscene or not it should be shown that the items were *utterly without any redeeming value*.[53] This made it possible to save a lot of items on the ground that although overtly sexy, they were not utterly without redeeming value. The *second* trend was demonstrated in a series of decisions of the American Supreme Court which suggested that obscenity laws should be directed against porn pushers and those who indulge in the commercial exploitation of sex.[54] To this was added the important caveat that children must be protected at all costs.[55]

The third trend was the privacy argument which was brought to the fore in the important decision of *Stanley* v. *Georgia*[56] which we have already discussed.

All these three trends suggested, as one writer put it, 'the requiem of *Roth*'.[57] But in June 1973, these trends came to be questioned in a series of eight decisions.[58] These decisions made clear that the right test was not 'the utterly without redeeming value' test and that it was important to consider the obscenity content of indicted items not by national standards but by local community standards.[59] Along with this, in another decision, an important clarification was made with respect to the doctrine of privacy.[60] It was stated very clearly that the doctrine in *Stanley* was limited to material read at home and did not create a zone of privacy which moved along with the individual wherever he went.[61] All of a sudden *Roth* was alive and well.

This saga which lasted seventeen years demonstrates how important it is to draft a Bill of Rights in such a way that ambiguities can be anticipated right from the start. Such an approach was followed in India where the article in question reads as follows:

19. *Protection of certain rights regarding freedom of speech, etc.*
   (1) All citizens shall have the right –

(a) to freedom of speech and expression . . . .
(2) Nothing in sub-clause (a) of clause (1) shall affect the operation of any existing law, or prevent the State from making any law, in so far as such law imposes reasonable restrictions on the exercise of the right conferred by the said sub-clause in the interests of . . . public order, decency or morality.

But, here too, when the article came to be considered in the prosecution of *Lady Chatterley's Lover,* the Supreme Court of India was able to use a protection argument in the face of a clearly laid down libertarian guaranteed right.[62] The important point that is demonstrated by this example is that in addition to a Bill of Rights model, it is also important to design a criminal law model in such a way that criminal law statutes directed against obscene items are drafted with sufficient procedural and substantive safeguards.

(c) *Pre-publication Censorship Models*
The procedure by which items are found to be obscene is almost as important as the substantive issue as of whether there should be any obscenity laws at all. It is important to select a process which provides certainty and at the same time accurately reflects what the law-maker intends.

For somebody using the direct protection model the answer is quite simple. He merely has to outline a well-drafted criminal law statute which will leave little room for the vagaries of interpretation. But the answer is not so simple if he wants to introduce either a libertarian element based on democratic notions of what the people want or a pre-publication warning system.

Should certain libertarian notions enter, the no-control approach (except in matters of children) and the indirect protection argument designed to prevent the commercial exploitation of sex and indiscriminate advertisement ought to be considered. But if the aim is to clamp down on indiscriminate advertisements and commercial exploitation, the best way to resolve the problem is to use a criminal law model and outlaw such practices. The alternative would be to ask the publishers either to show tremendous responsibility in this area or to institutionalise their responsibilities by creating an unofficial Ombudsman who would hear complaints. This would inevitably be a rather inefficient institution.

It could be said that expert opinion is needed. There are many ways in which the opinion of experts can be used. The first technique is that used in Section 4 of the Obscene Publications Act, 1959. By this method experts may give evidence on the literary, scientific and artistic merit of a book or publication. Their opinion may weigh with the court and save the book or publication even though it is found to be obscene. The second method was suggested by an American Supreme Court judge when he thought that there should be a special Court of Appeal simply to deal with matters related to obscenity laws.[63] The third method of dealing with expert evidence is to use official (as in New Zealand) or unofficial (as with films in England) pre-publication censorship boards. Thus, we have a choice between two institutional alternatives – the first is the use of a court, which is either itself expert or which is aided by experts; the second is to use expert pre-publication censorship boards. Many would argue that both these methods should be used but that more credibility would be given in a law court to the views of the pre-publication board.

A further and totally different approach would be to leave the matter in the hands of local councils. The object of this approach is that instead of the courts conducting an empirical inquiry into contemporary standards, these standards are themselves expressed through the views and votes of local councillors. Many artists would argue that this would introduce a political element into the decision-making process so that it becomes an unrefined political decision rather than a fair estimate either of what the artist wants or of what the people regard as respectable and acceptable. There is a lot in the English experience with respect to the cinema and local councils that lends support to this criticism.

Summing up

To sum up I will outline again my personal conclusions from this debate. First there is a need for greater research into the impact of the media so that legislation can be promulgated to control its effects. Secondly, some kind of philosophical preference has to be expressed between a 'no control' standpoint and either the direct protection argument or the indirect protection commercial/advertisement argument. It is also necessary to show empirically that one's standpoint can be supported by sociological and psychological evidence which demonstrates either the safety of the 'no control' position or the genuine vulnerability of society. The present writer believes that both philosophically and empirically the only case made out so far is for the need to tackle the danger of commercial exploitation of obscene items or their indiscriminate advertisement, rather than their creation or consumption. Thirdly, it would be advantageous to institute an official board which classifies items and establishes a system of pre-warning. The composition of this board should be fairly broad and its opinion should carry at least some persuasive weight in legal proceedings. Fourthly, assuming the need for limited protection to the extent stipulated by the indirect protection commercial/advertisement argument, there should be a use of a criminal law model which clearly states its objectives. If this is done a Bill of Rights technique should not be necessary.

In some ways the system put forward here – that of a criminal law approach directed against commercialisation of porn and overt acts of advertisement, based on the classifications of an unofficial board – might justly be defined as the death of civil liberties. After all, it involves a hard criminal law and establishes a system of pre-publication censorship. But this system is at least better than the existing one. The hard criminal law would be directed against those who exploit allegedly obscene items for commercial gain. Similarly, the pre-publication censorship system is really no more than a warning for those who both want and need a warning system to operate. These are the artist, the writer and the publisher. No matter how clumsy and cumbersome the suggestions may be, their effect is to make an individual free to read what he likes and see what he likes. His choice will be a free choice – uninfluenced by the insidious effect of indiscriminate advertisements or the alluring persistence of the porn pusher.

NOTES AND REFERENCES

1. A phrase taken from D. G. T. Williams: 'The Control of Obscenity' *Criminal Law Review* (1965), 522 at 530. Some M.P.s considering the *Unsolicited Goods and Services Bill,* seem to think that reputable publishers have no real problems (see *Times,* 19 March 1971).
2. e.g. *John Calder (Publications) Ltd.* v. *Powell* (1965) 1 Q.B. 509 (drugs); *D.P.P.* v. *A.B.C. Chewing Gum* (1968) 1 Q.B. 151 (violence). On the former see D. G. T. Williams (*supra* n.1); on the latter see G. Zellick: 'Violence as pornography' (1970) *Criminal Law Review* 188 and 199–200.
3. see *Blackburn* v. *Attorney General* (1971) 1 W.L.R. 1037.

4. see *Pornography – The Longford Report,* Coronet, London (1972), generally. Consider the Duke of Edinburgh's argument that excessive permissiveness led to excessive repression later (*Times* 21 November 1970). The basis of various protection arguments are discusssed in J. Miller: *Censorship and the limits of permission* (Sixth Annual Lecture under the Thank Offering British Fund 20 October 1971 – *O.U.P.* for the British Academy, 1972.

5. J. H. Court: 'Pornography and Sex Crimes' in V. Cline (ed.) *Where do you draw the line* (1975); see also article by M. Whitehouse *Sunday Times* 26 January 1975, and correspondence 2, 16, 23 February and 2 March 1975, *Sunday Times.*

6. H. J. Eysenck: 'Psychology and Obscenity – a factual look at some of the problems.' p. 148ff.

7. B. Kutchinsky: 'The effect of easy availability of pornography on the incidence of sex crimes: The Danish Experience' 29 *Jnl. of Social Issues* 163 (1973). Note the arguments of Alex Lyon in *The Times* 14 April 1973, p. 13.

8. *ibid:* see the figures at pp. 164–6.

9. It will be noted that special statutes govern the position of children, e.g. Section 1 of the *Children and Young Persons Act, 1955.*

10. *D.P.P.* v. *A.B.C. Chewing Gum (supra* n. 2).

11. For some philosophical arguments see G. Anastaplo: 'Obscenity and common sense: Towards a definition of 'community' and 'individuality' *St. Louis Univ. Law Journal* 16 (1972) pp. 527–56.

12. Planning statutes do not always cater for this directly; but aesthetic considerations are not unimportant. On planning see D. G. Smith' 'The progress and style of structural planning in England: Some observations' *Local Government Studies* 21, (1974).

13. *In re X (A minor): Wardship jurisdiction* (1975) 2 W.L.R. 335 (per Latey J.).

14. See H. Street: *Torts,* Butterworths (1967) Chapter 16 generally. In this case (*supra* n. 13) the defamation point was discussed in appeal by Lord Denning M.R. at p. 343.

15. *supra* n. 14 at 341 ff.

16. see Section 4, *Obscene Publications Act, 1959.* Thus a book declared to be 'obscene' under Section 1 could still be saved under Section 4.

17. see *Miller* v. *State of California* (1973) 41 *U.S.L.W.* 4925 at 4929 col. 2.

18. see the *New Zealand Indecent Publications Act, 1963.*

19. see *The Cinematograph Acts,* 1909–52.

20. *Miller* v. *State of California (supra* n. 17). An alternative would be to consider survey evidence see J. M. H. Lamont: 'Public Opinion Pools and survey evidence in obscenity cases' *Criminal Law Quarterly* (1973) 135.

21. *Miller* v. *State of California (supra* n. 17) at 4930 col. 2. 'People in different States vary in their tastes and attitudes and this diversity is not to be strangled by the absolutism of imposed uniformity'.

22. On the criminal law model consider the arguments of R. M. Jackson: 'Law of Obscenity' in Arts Council Working Party: *The Obscenity Laws* (Andre Deutsch, 1969) 71 and 73 that the criminal law model is not used to prevent harm but to support and maintain various conceptions of acceptable conduct.

23. see R. Dahrendorf *Essays in the Theory of Society,* Routledge and Kegan Paul, London (1968).

24. The literature on privacy is considerable. For some philosophical aspects see N. MacCormick: 'Privacy and Obscenity'.This volume, p. 76. For a discussion following United States Supreme Court rulings consider A. Katz: 'Privacy and Pornography: Stanley *v.* Georgia' (1969) *Sup. Ct. Rev.* 203.

25. *Stanley* v. *Georgia* (1969) 394 *U.S.* 557 at 564.

26. *U.S.* v. *37 Photographs* (1971) 402 *U.S.* 363. Note how *Stanley* v. *Georgia* (*supra* n. 25) is distinguished at p. 376; *U.S.* v. *Reidel* (1971) 402 *U.S.* 351.

27. *Paris Adult Theatre* v. *Slaton* (1973) 41 *U.S.L.W.* 4935.

28. *ibid:* at 4940–1 We have declined to equate the privacy of the home relied on in *Stanley* with a zone of privacy that follows a distributor or a consumer of obscene materials wherever he goes . . . The idea of privacy right and place of public accommodation are in this context, mutually exclusive. Conduct or depictions of conduct that the state police power can prohibit on a public street do not become automatically protected by the Constitution merely because the conduct is moved to a bar or a live theatre stage, any more than a live performance of a man and a woman locked in sexual embrace at high noon in Times Square is protected by the Constitution because they simultaneously engage in a valid political dialogue.

29. The question of Britain getting a Bill of Rights and entrenching it has been the subject of considerable discussion; see Sir Leslie Scarman: *English Law – The New Dimension* (1975) 69, 76–7, 81–3; Sir Keith Joseph: *Freedom under the Law* (Conservative Political Centre, 1975); Michael Zander: *A Bill of Rights* (1975); Lord Lloyd: 'Do we need a Bill of Rights' (1976) 39 *Mod. L.R.* 121; J. Jaconelli: 'The European Convention on Human Rights – The Text of a British Bill of Rights' (1976) *Public Law* 226.

30. The First Amendment, *Constitution of the United States of America.* For the extreme view that the Constitution does not admit of any control at all see Douglas J., *inter alia,* in *Miller* v. *State of California* (*supra* n. 17) at 4932–3.

31. see Article 19 (2) *Constitution of India,* 1950.

32. On local councils see E. Wistrich: 'Censorship and the Local Authority' (1974) *Local Government Studies* 1. For a defence of local authorities see G. Phelps: 'The Role and Problems of Local Government Film Censorship' (1974) *ibid* 11.

33. Note the effects of the *Obscene Publications Act,* 1959 Sections 1–2.

34. *supra,* n. 2.

35. *supra,* n. 2.

36. As for example the British Board of Film censors. On the working of this Board see J. Trevelyan: *What the Censor Saw* (1973) generally.

37. I am grateful for this information to the staff of Ulster Television.

38. see *Attorney General Reference (No. 2 of 1975),* (1976) 2 *All E.R.* 753.

39. The Arts Council Working Party (*supra* n. 22). The conclusions (pp. 33–5) do, however, suggest that the Film Board should continue.

40. Rutherford Ward: 'Books in the Dock' (1971) 6 May, *New Society* 777.

41. see G. Zellick: 'A new approach to the control of obscenity' (1970) 33 *Mod. L.R.* 289.

42. Section 10 of the *New Zealand Indecent Publications Act,* 1963.

43. This is the logic of the 'deprave and corrupt' formula which has been included in the definition of obscenity (see Section 1 of the *Obscene Publications Act*, 1959). Note that this is not necessarily the definition to be followed in all cases. See *R.* v. *Greater London Council ex. p. Blackburn* (1976) 3 *All E.R.* 184 on the definition to be followed by local councils. On the interpretation of the 'deprave and corrupt' formula see *D.P.P.* v. *Whyte* (1972) 3 *W.L.R.* 410.

44. see *D.P.P.* v. *A.B.C. Chewing Gum* (1968) 1 Q.B. 159 at 165.

45. *R.* v. *Anderson* (1971) 3 *W.L.R.* 939 at 946. For a sample of how various psychiatrists view their own expert evidence consider the views of the 'sex perts' S. Crane, C. Brook, C. Pickard, M. Yaffe in *Sunday Times Magazine* 14 November 1976, pp. 32–3.

46. *R.* v. *Staniforth; R.* v. *Jordan* (1976) 2 *All E.R.* 714 that the therapeutic value of porn is no longer really a relevant matter under Section 4 of the *Obscene Publications Act,* 1959.

47. e.g. Section 4, *The Vagrancy Act,* 1824; Section 2, *The Vagrancy Act,* 1838; Section 28, *Town Police Clauses Act,* 1847; Section 42, *Customs Consolidation Act,* 1876; Section 3, The *Indecent Advertisements Act,* 1889; Section 11, *Post Office Act,* 1953; Section 1, *The Children and Young Persons (Harmful Publications) Act*; (The text of the above has been collected in the Arts Council Working Party Report (*supra* n. 22).

48. see *Shaw* v. *D.P.P.* (1961) A.C. 220; *R.* v. *Knuller (Publishing, Printing and Promotions) Ltd.* (1971) 3 *W.L.R.* 663 (C.A.) (1973) A.C. 435.

49. see *R.* v. *Straker* (1965) *Criminal Law Review* 239; *R.* v. *Stanley* (1965) 2 *W.L.R.* 917.

50. *The Theatres Act,* 1968.

51. *supra* n. 35.

52. *Roth* v. *United States* (1957) 354 *U.S.* 476.

53. e.g. Brennan J. in *A Book . . .* v. *Attorney General* (1966) 383 *U.S.* 413 at 418.

54. e.g. *Ginsberg* v. *United States* (1966) 383 *U.S.* 463; *Mishkin* v. *United States* (1966) 383 *U.S.* 502.

55. *Ginsberg* v. *New York* (1968) 390 U.S. 629. See further: S. Krislov: 'From Ginzburg to Ginsberg: The unhurried children's hour in obscenity legislation' (1968) *Sup. Ct. Rev.* 153; Note: 'A double standard of Obscenity: The Ginsberg decision' (1968). 3 *Val Univ. L.R.* 57; Note: 'Constitutional Law – Obscenity – Materials may be obscene for minors without being obscene for adults' (1968) 21 *Vand. L.R.* 844.

56. (1969) *supra* n. 30.

57. D. E. Engdahl: 'Requiem for Roth: Obscenity doctrine is changing' (1969) 68 *Michigan L.R.* 185 and note the reply S. K. Laughlin Jnr. 'A Requiem for Requiems: The Supreme Court at the Bar of reality' (1970) 68 *Michigan L.R.* 1389.

58. *Miller* v. *State of California* (*supra* n. 21): *Paris Adult Theatre* v. *Slaton* (*supra* n. 27); *United States* v. *Orito* (1973) 41 U.S.L.W. 4956; *Kaplan* v. *State of California* (1973) *ibid* 4958; *United States* v. *Twelve two-hundred Foot Reels of Super Eight Millimeter Film* (1973) *ibid* 4961; *Heller* v. *State of New York* (1973) *ibid* 5067; *Roaden* v. *State of Kentucky* (1973) *ibid* 5070; *Alexander* v. *State of Virginia* (1973) *ibid* 5074.

59. *Miller* v. *State of California* (*supra* n. 21).

60. As enunciated in *Stanley* v. *State of Georgia* (*supra* n. 30).

61. *Paris Adult Theatre* v. *Slaton* (*supra* n. 27).

62. *Ranjit Udeshi* v. *State of Maharashtra* A.I.R. 1956 S.C. 881.

63. A suggestion made by Justice Black and referred to in the preliminary *Report of the Presidential Commission on Pornography* (1970).

Privacy and Obscenity

by D. N. MacCormick

Is there any legally or morally significant connection between the topics of privacy and of obscenity? Does respect for the privacy of individuals tell in favour of banning obscene publications, or in favour of abolishing legal restrictions on the use or dissemination of obscene materials? Is legislative prohibition of obscene publications calculated to protect or to infringe the right of individuals to privacy (so far as they have such a right either in law or in morality)?

These are the questions which will be considered and explored in this paper. From the outset a paradox, or at least an apparent paradox, must be faced. The paradox is that it appears possible either to argue that respect for privacy requires a regime of freedom in relation to the use and enjoyment of obscene materials, or to argue that respect for privacy requires legal controls upon their use and dissemination. Indeed, it may be possible to advance both arguments at the same time, by contending that up to a certain point the right of privacy entails a right to freedom from restraint in the use of obscene materials, but that beyond that point some legal restraints are required in the interests of privacy.

The best proof that it is possible to advance such arguments is to show that they have been advanced by people whose views are, on the face of it, worth some respect. To do so is of course not to demonstrate that all or any of the arguments are soundly based, but it will pave the way for considering critically and in a fresh light what, if any, are the genuine bearings of privacy on obscenity and vice versa. Such critical consideration is the business of this paper, so let the way be paved for it forthwith.

My source of arguments for preliminary consideration is a series of recent decisions given by the U.S. Supreme Court in various cases involving review of prosecutions of possessors, users, and publishers of things alleged to be obscene.

The first, the case of *Stanley* v. *Georgia* (1968),[1] concerned a conviction under a statute of the State of Georgia for 'Knowingly hav[ing] possession of . . . obscene matter', namely certain films found in his desk drawer during a search by federal and state agents in his home under a warrant authorising them to search for materials relating to an illegal wagering business. The Supreme Court, reversing the decision of the court below, held that the First and Fourteenth Amendments prohibit making mere private possession of obscene material a crime, and that the Georgia Statute was unconstitutional.[2]

An important element in the justification of the ruling given was concern for the protection of privacy. As Marshall, J., giving the opinion of the Court, said, the First Amendment right to freedom of speech and of the press entails a right to receive information.

> This right to receive information and ideas, regardless of their social worth . . . is fundamental to our free society. Moreover, in the context of this case – a prosecution for mere possession of printed or filmed matter in the privacy of a person's own home – that right takes on an added dimension. For also fundamental is the right to be free, except in very limited circumstances, from unwanted governmental intrusions into one's privacy.[3]

And he went on later to say, 'Whatever may be the justifications for other statutes regulating obscenity, we do not think they reach into the privacy of one's own home.'[4]

Here, then, we have an example of an argument that recognition of a right of personal and domestic privacy, at least as a right associated with that of free speech and free access to ideas and information, is necessarily hostile to an attempted legislative prohibition on the possession or use of obscene materials. It is perhaps worth noticing, too, that the Court was careful to distinguish this area of activity from that of possession of 'other items, such as narcotics, firearms or stolen goods' which in its view could legitimately be made criminal wherever and however privately such items might be kept.[5]

In part, the significance of the ruling in *Stanley*'s case is precisely the way in which appeal to a right of individual privacy was used in setting a limit to the extent to which anti-obscenity laws can be held constitutional. This decision departed significantly from the judgment in the case of *Roth* v. *United States* (1957),[6] when it was held that 'obscenity is not within the area of constitutionally protected speech or press'.[7] The point of distinction was that *Roth* and similar precedents all involved some form of publication, or public distribution or dissemination, of materials deemed objectionable. One ground adduced as showing the materiality of the distinction between those activities and mere private possession is of particular interest for the present purpose: 'public distribution . . . is subject to different objections [from private possession]. For example, there is always the danger that obscene material . . . might intrude upon the sensibilities or privacy of the general public.'[8]

In that sentence can be seen a version of the opposite argument about privacy in relation to obscenity: whereas the right to privacy has been advanced as a reason for striking down legislation penalising the private possession of obscene articles, now the right of privacy is held to entail a right to protection from intrusion by publication of obscene materials. Thus, it appears, privacy may have a Janus-faced relevancy to penalties for obscenity, striking them down in relation to a person's private use and enjoyment of the obscene, backing them up in relation to a person's public dissemination of obscenity to others.

It is not obvious and it may appear self-contradictory to argue in this way that the claim of privacy may pull in two conflicting directions in relation to obscenity laws, since plainly there is a difference between my having 'dirty' books or pictures for my own private use and my disseminating them to other people; the idea behind the argument is that it would be an intrusion into my privacy for the state to take action in the former case, whereas in the latter my foisting the materials in question on to others is itself an intrusion upon theirs. But even if there is not contradiction there is at least a tension between the two arguments, in that one who accepts both, faces some problems of balancing. If my right of privacy involves a right to use and peruse materials of my own choosing, it is not (in this respect) worth much if I cannot lay hold of the kind of thing I like to peruse. But, on the whole, I cannot get hold of it unless I can acquire it, and I cannot without difficulty acquire it unless someone is disseminating it. Again, if he is passing it to me by my desire and with my consent, the privacy-based objection to trading in obscene articles appears on the face of it to have little force. So if there is (and it remains to be seen whether there is) anything in either the argument for or the argument against anti-obscenity laws so far as they are based on the right of, or the value of, privacy, it appears that at some point a balance has to be struck between the rights of privacy protected by prohibitions on obscenity and the competing rights of privacy infringed by such prohibitions. It does not look like an easy task to strike such a balance.

The experience of the U.S. Supreme Court, as evidenced most recently in a series of decisions handed down in June 1973, confirms that it is not easy. For example, in *U.S. v. 12 200ft. Reels, U.S. v. Orito*[9] the question was raised as to the constitutionality of Federal statutes prohibiting respectively the importation of, and the inter-state transportation of, obscene materials. In each case it was argued that since a person has a constitutional right to private possession even of materials judged obscene, he must have an ancillary right to bring such materials into the U.S.A. for his own private use, or to transport them from state to state for the like purpose; if he has that right, legislation prohibiting importation or interstate trans-portation of such material, unless it is limited to the case of importation for commercial purposes, must be unconstitutional. In both cases, the majority of the Court, led by C. J. Burger, rejected the argument.

Here is a sample of the reasoning:

> We are not disposed to extend the precise, carefully limited, holding of Stanley to permit importation of admittedly obscene materials simply because they are imported for private use only . . . We have already indicated that the protected right to possess obscene material in the privacy of one's home does not give rise to a correlative right to have someone sell or give it to others *(U.S. v. Thirty Seven Photographs)*[10] . . . Nor is there any correlative right to transport obscene material in interstate commerce *(U.S. v. Orito)*[11] It follows that Stanley does not permit one to go abroad and bring such material into the country for private purposes. 'Stanley's emphasis was on the freedom of thought and mind in the privacy of the home. But a port of entry is not a traveller's home' *(U.S. v. Thirty Seven Photographs)*.[12]

In both cases, and indeed in the whole series of recent decisions there were strong dissents from J. Douglas and J. Brennan, with the latter of whom Stewart and J. J. Marshall joined. The following passage from the opinion of J. Douglas, in the 12 200ft. Reels case, is characteristically pungent:

> Finally, it is ironic to me that in this Nation many pages must be written and many hours spent to explain why a person who can read whatever he desires, *Stanley v. Georgia* . . ., may not without violating the law carry

that literature in his briefcase or bring it from abroad. Unless there is that ancillary right, one's Stanley rights could be realised, as has been suggested, only if one wrote or designed a tract in his attic and printed or processed it in his basement, so as to be able to read it in his study.[13]

The general line of the (conservative) majority of the Court in the recent decision has been to give a very limited ambit to the privacy-based right of possession of or access to obscene material, restricting it indeed to the 'privacy of the home' principle. In the case of *Paris Adult Theatre I* v. *Slaton*[14] the majority gave a ruling that the right of privacy did not extend so far as to confer a protected right on consenting adults to pursue their own choice in the matter of watching obscene and pornographic motion pictures within a theatre which was not open to minors and which gave patrons due notice of the kind of entertainment provided. Accordingly, state statutes of Georgia prohibiting and penalising such exhibitions were not unconstitutional.

In justifying his decision, C. J. Burger quoted with approval from an article by Professor Bickel which again refers to the two-way pull of claims of privacy in relation to permission or prohibition of obscenity.

> A man may be entitled to read an obscene book in his room, or expose himself indefinitely there . . . We should protect his privacy. But if he demands a right to obtain the books and pictures he wants in the market, and to foregather in public places – discreet, if you will, but accessible to all – with others who share his tastes, *then to grant him his right is to affect the world about the rest of us and to impinge on other privacies*. Even supposing that each of us can, if he wishes, effectively avert the eye and stop the ear (which in truth, we cannot), what is commonly read and seen and heard and done intrudes upon us all, want it or not.[15]

Finally, to illustrate that the opinions and concerns expressed in the foregoing are not purely transatlantic in origin or focus, one may point to the report entitled *Pornography,* published by the 'Longford Committee'. On the one hand, the report notes as a possible 'evil' arising from anti-obscenity laws 'the invasion of privacy or an unjustifiable restriction of an individual's liberty of moral choice' and asserts that 'there would . . . seem to be weighty objections to any attempt to restrict by law what books an individual reads or pores over in privacy'. On the other hand, in the section on 'Conclusions and Recommendations', the Committee avers that 'an important aspect of what we have called the "problems" of pornography [is] the overruling of choice or invasion of privacy where sexual display cannot be avoided'.[16]

The foregoing section confronts us with instances of two potentially conflicting, but not self-evidently contradictory arguments: that respect for the privacy of individuals is inconsistent with the existence of laws against obscenity, at least in certain respects; and that respect for the privacy of individuals is a justifying reason for the existence of laws against obscenity, at least in certain respects. Can either or both of these arguments withstand critical examination? That is the question for discussion in the rest of this paper.

I propose to begin by considering the second-mentioned argument, that laws against obscenity are protective of privacy. As to that, the view for which I shall argue is that there is at best a very loose and indirect connection between restricting obscene displays, publications, etc. and protecting privacy. (Whether there are other, and better arguments for maintaining or for that matter strengthening, the law obscene publications is a question which I shall not pursue.)

In the not-very-recent past, a British philosopher might have been expected to deal with the question simply by demonstrating that the terms 'privacy' and 'obscenity' as they are used in common English speech (at least, in the speech of philosophers) are, in fact, used in different ways. From that demonstration, it would follow that the words have different meanings. If the words have different meanings, it follows that the right to privacy and the right to protection from obscene displays are different rights. As a matter of observation, I am inclined to think that the premise is true; but I doubt if it will bear the weight of the conclusion which depends upon it.

Even if it is true that ordinary English speakers do not make any very close connection between privacy and obscenity, that cannot supply a sufficient argument to show that the moral or legal reformer is unjustified in seeking to exhibit important analogies and similarities between the areas covered by the two terms, and in the light of those to argue that the good reasons supporting a right of privacy are equally good as supporting a right to protection from obscenity. That established, he may if he chooses go on to argue that the concept of a 'right of privacy' should be recognised as including within it a subsidiary right to protection from obscene displays, literature, etc. If there were important analogies and similarities between the two areas, then there could surely be nothing objectionable in this extension or development of linguistic conventions. There is an obvious danger of moral as well as linguistic conservatism in excessive worship of common usage. It will not do, therefore, to rest one's whole argument in such a field as this merely on an attempt to elucidate common usage.

What is clear is that any attempt to justify protection from obscenity as an instance of protection of privacy depends essentially upon the thesis that the same value, the same reasons of principle, are the underlying justifications of each form of protection. If that thesis is unacceptable it would merely be a form of mischievous obfuscation to treat protection from obscenity as an element in the protection of privacy. The attempted redefinition of terms would result solely in the introduction of a gratuitous equivocation into any argument about either privacy or obscenity. I believe the thesis to be false and shall forthwith set out my reasons for believing it so.

Let me start by asking what we protect when we protect privacy. What kind of legal right would a legal right to privacy be? I have asked and answered the same question before, and so may be tolerably brief here.[17] Our right to privacy, in so far as it is what is sometimes called a 'claim-right', is essentially a right to non-intrusion. As such, it must be a right to non-intrusion in some respect which can be specified. My right to domestic privacy, for example, is a right that no-one else shall intrude into my home or home life save by my invitation or permission. Such a right presupposes as correlative a duty incumbent on some other person or persons (indeed, in this case, all other persons) not to intrude upon me in the specified (or understood) way. To be rather exact about it, the right of privacy is a right which sustains a series of claims against a large, perhaps indefinite, group of other people all of whom owe me the duty not to intrude upon some aspect or aspects of my life and affairs.

To confer upon people legal protection of their privacy, is, in effect, to invest in them certain rights against other people, and to impose upon other people correlative duties of non-intrusion in the affairs of the people protected. Either in a strict, or at least in a metaphorical, sense privacy is always in some degree 'territorial'. That is to say, there is some sphere within which the individual is in the relevant sense protected from intrusion. The sphere in question may be some geographical area, such as his home or his office at work; or again, it may be the 'sphere' of his personal activities and interests which are protected from snooping or interference wherever he is. (It can be as much an invasion of privacy if a stranger in a train seeks to prise from one detailed personal information, as if somebody tries to do so on one's own front doorstep.)

'Intrusion' however is a wide concept. The burglar who ransacks my house, or the hoodlum who mugs me in the street, intrudes upon the security of my home, or, as the case may be, my person. In neither case, however, is the gist of his offence adequately captured by saying simply that he has invaded my privacy. To take something which belongs to me, or to injure me physically, albeit kinds of 'intrusion' are, I think, objectionable on other grounds than invading my privacy. To give an example, a burglar may break into my house and steal what he hopes is a valuable document; on leaving the house he discovers that it is nothing more than a personal diary which he has stolen, and in disgust he burns it without having scrutinised its contents at all. He is clearly guilty of theft, though I think not guilty of intruding upon my privacy as such. By contrast, a visitor to my house might perhaps take the opportunity of surreptitiously reading the contents of my private diary. Here there is neither theft, nor, at any rate in Scots law, any form of trespass. But there is, as most of us would say, a serious breach of personal privacy.

How then shall we account for these differences, and how shall we capture the notion of intrusion which is special to the case of privacy? The answer, as it appears to me, is that we must postulate the existence of a general human interest in being able for some purposes some of the time to 'keep oneself to oneself'. The basis of privacy is some kind of desire for seclusion. Taking our earlier concept of a 'sphere', we can say that within certain spheres at least some and probably all human beings desire to be able to seclude themselves. This desire for seclusion should not be construed in all cases as a desire to exclude all other human beings from one's life or some aspect of it; rather it is a desire to have the last say on which other human beings will be brought within the circle of one's seclusion for certain purposes. It has indeed been argued by some that the basis of a desire for privacy or a desire for seclusion is precisely that intimacy presupposes the possibility of seclusion.[18] I can make myself intimate with my friends or my wife or whomsoever, only given that I am granting to them some special privilege which is not shared by other people in general. Real relationships of love, friendship and trust are created by the sharing of intimacy within areas of life which we do in fact ordinarily keep secluded from other people.

To the extent that any individual in respect of some area or aspect of his life takes steps to exclude all or most other people and/or demands that others concede him seclusion, to that extent we may say that he asserts '*de facto*' privacy. Plainly not all claims to *de facto* privacy are such as would be generally regarded as legitimate. A private meeting of the heads of Mafia families might be one which the 'public interest' would be best served by busting. But in the light of legal or moral norms it may be that some claims to *de facto* privacy are recognised as being legitimate claims. It is hard to imagine any viable system of positive morality within which no claims to privacy are recognised as legitimate, although it is easy to point to legal systems which do not grant a parallel legal right.

These reflections suggest that rights to privacy, (in addition to entailing a series of claims against all other human beings), being claims against intrusion, also entail a 'normative power'[19] possessed by each individual, to waive his claims in respect to individuals chosen by him. These are to the extent of his permission admitted within his circle of intimacy in some particular matter or 'sphere'. That helps us to specify the particular forms of intrusion against which the right avails. It is that intrusion which consists in seeking to know about or to observe or to find out about an individual in those contexts in which he desires that knowledge about himself or observation of himself and his activities should be restricted either absolutely or to those alone to whom he himself reveals such knowledge, or whom he admits to watching him lounging in his armchair, or whatever.[20]

It seems to me likely that the matter of privacy is, in many ways, culturally relative. The spheres within which people actively desire self-seclusion, and the spheres within which a common social morality concedes the legitimacy of self-seclusion, may indeed vary greatly from time to time. What is more, there may be from time to time and from place to place wider or narrower ranges of desire for privacy or of the concession of the legitimacy of some aspect of privacy.

There seems indeed to be abundant evidence for some degree of cultural relativity in these matters. There is probably even very considerable difference between different social sub-groups within a larger society. It may well be for example that desire for and respect of privacy are more keenly felt among certain segments of middle class society in contemporary Britain than in other strata of society.[21]

All that this would amount to saying, however, is that there are some crucial cultural variables within what is a quite general concept of privacy.

It seems on the face of it by no means unlikely that for any individual and for any society there will be some areas within which there is both a general (and perhaps socially implanted) desire for seclusion and a general concession of the reasonableness of such desire. There is so much which seems to depend on the possibility of seclusion that one is almost inevitably driven to this conclusion. I have mentioned earlier the notion that intimacy with some people presupposes a possibility of excluding all others. To that one may add the perhaps general desire in most people to 'be themselves' some of the time, as distinct from playing some public role, as they do, and desire to do, at other times. We all, it seems, have a need for some degree of autonomy, some degree of self-regulation, unimpeded and uninfluenced by the demands or judgments or even detached observation of other human beings.

I have suggested, and I can see reason to believe, that such desires are very generally felt by human beings. But the thesis that all people ought to have and to be recognised as having a right to privacy in at least some of the spheres in which privacy can be exercised is not dependent on empirical evidence as to how many people (if any) actively desire it at a given time in a given society. It is sufficient for the justification of that thesis that we should judge autonomy of this kind, together with the possibility of 'power over intimacy' as being values important in themselves. There is nothing wrong with conferring or recognising human rights to things which not everyone (even not many people) wants; for, or course, to have a right is, normally, to have the option whether one exercises it or not. Those who don't want privacy are in no way inconvenienced by being given a right to it. If they don't want others to have privacy, the question is whether their wish in that matter is legitimate; at which point we come back to the value question, not to an empirical question. All this is true whether we have in mind the recognition of a moral right or the conferment of a legal right.

To that extent I think that there are grounds for arguing that (even if the desire for privacy were not entirely general) there would be good reason for conceding some degree of seclusion to every human being whatsoever, and for recognising a right to such seclusion. There are doubtless many ways of making and arguing such points as these, and there is indeed a most voluminous literature exploring such arguments. I shall not take the argument any further here. To sum it all up: when a right of privacy in some respect or respects is granted or conceded to all individuals within the range of some normative system (legal or moral), the recognition or grant of that right creates a sphere of or individual (or it may be of small group) autonomy. Within the sphere acknowledged, the individual (or the small group) has the right of choice, the right of admission or exclusion of observation or knowledge or 'joining in' by others. Some may value such autonomy more, others may value it less; but the value upon which privacy rests is, surely, the value of autonomy in shaping a personal, as distinct from a public, dimension of one's life. The wrong of intrusion is the wrong of infringing that aspect of an individual's autonomy contrary to his wish and without his permission.

If the argument presented above is acceptable, it follows that the right (if any) to be protected from obscenity can be subsumed under the right to protection from intrusion upon privacy only if there is some substantial and important sense in which the former protection can be seen as furthering the claim of autonomy in the way in which protection of privacy furthers it. To say the least, it would be hard to sustain that argument.

At any rate if one starts by considering the somewhat tendentious legal definition of obscenity which characterises it in terms of its tendency to produce effects (depraving and corrupting) which no sound evidence has shown that it does produce, the wrong done to an individual who is exposed to some obscene production does not seem in any way more analogous to the wrong of breach of privacy than is the already mentioned case of wronging a person either by stealing his property or assaulting his person. It may be said that to deprave and corrupt somebody is to deprive him of the possibility to make a good use of his autonomy; but to kill somebody or to assault him so seriously that he is hospitalised, is equally, or more, to deprive him of the capacity of using his autonomy, for ever or for some time. Equally, if you steal my car, you deprive me of one place in which to have private conversations with my associates (I do indeed believe that automobiles are occasionally used as the sites of other forms of activity at least as private as conversation); but you do not *eo ipso* invade my privacy.

What is more, if one departs from the rather tendentious legal definition of obscenity, and if one considers the cognate notions of obscenity and indecency without regard to their alleged effects, one finds that their gist concerns the doing in public what ought not to be done in public if at all. There is probably a line to be drawn between sexual and sadistic obscenity and indecency. The former consists in making public display of things the public display of which is held to be objectionable though the private existence or practice of them is unobjectionable. Sadistic obscenity and indecency depict or display acts of violence and cruelty which ought not to be practised at all.

If the essence of obscenity and indecency is the public revelation, display, depiction, or description of such matters, there is on the face of it some oddity in subsuming such conduct within the rubric of intruding upon other people's privacy. It appears that those who indulge themselves in obscene displays or whatever are rather waiving their own privacy than impeding or intruding upon that of others. Indeed it seems as if that which is willingly done in public falls outside the sphere of any individual's privacy. We have noted earlier how the concept of privacy involves drawing a literal or metaphorical sphere around each individual person; within that sphere he has a choice whom, if anyone, to admit to intimacy with him. As with all concepts of seclusion or exclusion, the drawing of such lines of seclusion presupposes that there is something, as it were, on the other side of the line. What is not within the special power of any particular individual lies within the general domain in which all are free to take as much or as little interest as they choose without regard to the desires of others. I may be shocked, horrified or titillated against my wishes by matters which other people choose to bring into the public arena. I may experience such shock, horror or titillation as offences; but the offence is not the offence of intrusion into my sphere of privacy. What is more, so long as I have the right and the freedom to avert my gaze or go elsewhere, the offence is one which I can escape precisely by availing myself of my own privacy.

There is an objection to this line of argument which, if well founded, would be fatal to it. If people, as they go about their daily business in public places, are confronted on cinema hoardings or news-stands or wherever with materials which they find offensively obscene, is that not, from their point of view, a kind of 'intrusion' into their private consciousness, a thrusting-in of undesired images and thoughts? And if so, is this not then one form of invasion of privacy as contended by Professor Bickel in the passage cited above.[22]

The last thing which I would wish to deny is that people may well feel such a sense of offence as is here mentioned, perhaps even to the extent of finding their freedom to go about the public streets constrained and restricted, in that one has to choose whether to sustain serious offence or to keep away from certain parts of the town. But for my part, I cannot see this as a question of privacy, if only because at that rate almost every aspect of one's concern for one's environment would involve an element of concern for privacy. If a beautiful old Georgian terrace is torn down and a brutal concrete tower block substituted for it, some people may be deeply offended by that, and may even feel obliged to stay away from the place rather than sustain the offence. Or if the garbage collection services were removed from part of the town, so that it became smelly and unhealthy, or if raw sewage were wantonly pumped into a beautiful river, such conditions would be very offensive to most of us.

But what all that shows is that we have a legitimate interest in a tasteful, salubrious and healthy environment, not that our interest in it is the same as our interest in privacy, or an element in it. Even given the degree of figurativeness which I am willing to admit in the notion of 'intrusion' into a 'sphere' of privacy, I do think that it would be stretching things to the point where the concept loses all its distinctive utility if we were to extend our conception of privacy to include all aspects of environmental offence. And if we don't include them all, I cannot see the rationale of including one, that of the offence provided by publicly displayed obscene articles. So I remain unconvinced by the objection.

It is sometimes said that obscene matter in television broadcasts and the like may amount to an invasion of privacy, in the case of a viewer who dislikes such matter, and does not wish it to be thrust into his home. The argument is a bad one, since one has a simple method of 'averting one's gaze' viz., by switching off. All the same points can be made as will shortly be made in relation to mail, but in a stronger form, since one has the option of not owning or possessing a T.V. receiver.

There is a different and interesting, argument, that public service broadcasting, supported from public funds (i.e. the B.B.C. particularly) should not use the public's money to produce what the public doesn't want. 'I pay my licence fee in order to get programmes I like in my own house, not this rubbish.' Interesting and important arguments about democracy and accountability of public bodies arise here, and there are (at least) two sides to the argument. But it would be a blatant case of 'persuasive definition' for either side to claim support on the ground of the 'right to privacy'.

Indeed, in general terms, it appears to me that whatever offence there is in the areas of obscenity and indecency, it can only be characterised as offence against everyone in general and no-one in particular (though this is subject to exceptions which will be considered). The analogies of obscenity and indecency are most clearly and closely to be found in such areas as breach of the peace, public nuisance, environmental pollution and the like. Somebody who pollutes an estuary does not harm anybody in particular; he harms 'the public in general'. That may be a harm amply sufficient to justify prohibitions and penalties. But it would surely be a mistake to view the offence as an invasion of the right of any individual in particular. Public nuisance and private nuisance are plainly distinguishable.

In this respect one finds an entire distinction from the case of invasion of privacy. Although there may be good general utilitarian reasons why the privacy of each and every person should be respected, every manifestation of breach of privacy is breach of some specific individual's privacy. In so far as there are laws protecting privacy, and in so far as those laws are to the general good, the general good is secured by protecting individuals severally. By contrast, in the case of, say, environmental pollution, the general good is directly secured by prohibiting certain activities which are considered harmful to the community at large even though there may be no indentifiable and specific harm to any specific person. At any rate indentifiable and specific injury to a particular person is not essential to the offence. Students of jurisprudence will readily recognise here a tacit reference to John Austin's famous distinction between absolute and relative duties.[23] It is submitted that Austin made a perfectly valid point in drawing that distinction, whether or not each and every instance which he mentions as a case of the distinction is well conceived.

As has been conceded in advance there are exceptions to the general point just made. The exceptions, however, on scrutiny rather support than weaken the case put. Let us suppose that a magazine publishes a photograph of a man and a woman in the act of sexual intercourse. Let us further suppose that the photograph has been obtained illicitly by the unkown and unpermitted use of a surveillance device in a private bedroom. The individuals whose photograph is displayed are plainly the victims of a breach of their privacy. There is nothing wrong with their activity; there is everything wrong with uninvited surveillance of it, and the wrong is compounded by the publicisation of the visual image. A similar case may be made out in relation to what may be called exploitative obscenity. If it is the case that severe economic or other pressures can be put upon actors and actresses or photographic models to secure that they unwillingly participate in public displays of an indecent or an obscene character, then, to the extent that their consent was not really free consent, they have suffered an infringement of their privacy. They have been forced into a position of making public that which they would not otherwise have wished to make public.

But in each case the element of intrusion is entirely separate from the element of obscenity or indecency. If we consider the case of persons who of their own free consent, without either duress or illicit observation, permit precisely such displays of themselves as those already considered, the resultant photographs may be indistinguishable from a visual point of view. If either set of pictures is obscene or offensive, both are, considered simply in themselves. In the former case there has been an offence against specific individuals as well as the postulated offence to people in general resulting from publication. In the latter case the element of offence to specific individuals is missing but the public offensiveness of the display is neither greater nor less.

Another, at least arguable, exception is presented in rather different vein by the instance of delivery by mail of unsolicited obscene materials of an advertising or indeed of any other kind. To the extent that such materials are deposited in people's houses without their desire, consent or invitation, that constitutes an intrusion on privacy. But non-obscene materials cascading through one's letter-box can be just as intrusive. The fact is that the existence of a postal service facilitates a minor form of intrusion into people's homes, to the extent that outsiders can pester them with materials which they do not wish to receive or see. Perhaps many people strongly dislike obscene materials. But it is specifically the undesired rather than the obscene quality of the mail which makes it intrusive. (Consider the converse case of the person who likes and hopes to get unsolicited obscene material but who can't stand political pamphlets.)

It seems to follow from what has been said that offensive obscenity and offensive intrusions on privacy are entirely different categories and types of wrong except for the areas of overlap in which the production of obscene materials may involve intrusion in other people's private affairs either without their consent or at least without their free and willing consent. It seems therefore that it must be wrong to treat any case of obscenity as such (apart from the issue of the means of obtaining obscene material) as being a wrong (if wrong at all) of a similar kind to breach of privacy.

There is perhaps one line of argument which might be advanced as supporting some degree of connection between respect for privacy and repression of obscenity, at any rate by way of obscene publications or public displays. It might be said that the essence of obscenity lies in some gross breach of flagration of those standards of decency or modesty which are held in a given society or social group. No doubt such standards are variable, and do vary, from place to place and from time to time, and no doubt legal moralists are much too prone to considering that for even large and complex societies it is possible to find or to prescribe some single set of common standards of modesty and decency. But having expressed all due reservations, it seems true as a matter of common observation that some standards of decency and modesty in sexual and other matters are observed in almost all groups, and that their being observed is thought important. Whatever may be the justification of such standards and conventions, there too is to be found whatever justification there may be for prohibitions on obscene displays and publications (therein, too, if anywhere, is to be found a workable definition of obscenity, if definition be desired). But has all that anything to do with privacy?

Very tentatively, I should suggest that there may be some connection between respect for such standards and respect for privacy. Given that standards of modesty are indeed changeable and changing, and that they may be more or less extensive, rather as clothing may be longer or shorter according to fashions of different times, it might be argued that recognition of and respect for duties of modesty can lend support to individuals' claims for privacy. If there is some range of emotions, activities etc. which one is expected not to disclose or display in public, those who do wish to keep themselves to themselves in such matters may have an easier task in asserting their right to do so than they would in a society in which more or less 'anything goes'. There may at least be some concomitance in attitudes as between an attitude of respect for people's privacy and an attitude of respect for norms of decency and modesty in sexual and other matters. And it may be that respect for modesty and decency requires the support of some kind of legal regulation of the obscene. But, as is obvious, the connection here with privacy is at best tenuous, and is in any event only tentatively suggested. It seems that a sound justification of anti-obscenity laws will need to be based on stronger and more directly apposite grounds than this somewhat tenuous link between attitudes of respect for privacy and attitudes of hostility to obscenity, indecency and immodesty.

Among the reasons for adopting a cautious and tentative view of this last-mentioned argument is the rather obvious consideration that the preceding discussion led to the conclusion that it is a form of individual autonomy which is the basic underlying value essentially involved in recognition of a right of privacy. The freedom to be oneself, to choose one's own intimates, and to choose how far, if at all, certain aspects of one's thoughts and activities and way of life in general should be opened to others is the core of liberty which the right of privacy protects at the perimeter. But if that is so, any legal or moral restrictions upon one's choice to keep things to oneself or impart them to others is a restriction which conflicts with the underlying principles on which recognition of a right to privacy is founded. There may be independent and forceful reasons for requiring people to keep private matters – or indeed private parts – private, but I cannot believe that such requirements can be founded on the same principles as those which may move us to recognise or to assert a right of privacy. The protection of privacy is essentially an aspect of the protection of individual freedom of choice, of choice what kind of person to be. The discouragement or restriction or prohibition of obscenity is a limitation on freedom of choice, limiting in some areas one's choice as to the kinds of things one does, whether or not one sees them as expressing the kind of person one wants to be. Such restrictions cannot therefore be credibly justified on grounds of protecting privacy, whatever other grounds may be advanced in support of them.

And so we are back to the considerations which moved the Supreme Court in *Stanley* v. *Georgia*. For by contrast with the attempt to use the value of privacy as a support for anti-obscenity laws, an attempt which must fail, the assertion that protection of privacy involves protection from such laws is vindicated by the considerations most recently advanced. The kind of respect for individual autonomy which is manifested in recognition of individual rights of privacy, demands as a minimum the degree of freedom from supervision or restriction upon one's private reading, viewing and acting which the Supreme Court held to be constitutionally entrenched in *Stanley*'s case. Whatever else one may doubt, one can surely entertain no doubt that state or other public regulation of the contents of an individual's personal library or his collection of pictures, films or records and the like would be fundamentally inconsistent with recognition of any worthwhile right of individual privacy. Here, surely, we find an uncomplicated instance of John Stuart Mill's conception of self-regarding acts and activities in relation to which public regulation of individual taste would be wholly contrary to quite fundamental rights of freedom and autonomy.

It is not clear that any ground of principle worth serious consideration can be advanced against extension of such a claim based on privacy to cover the case of one's personal and private possessions wherever one may for the moment have them, whether in one's brief-case on a train, in a car on a journey, or packed in a removal lorry or a freight carrying plane. The limits recently set by the U.S. Supreme Court restricting *Stanley* ruling to the narrow ambit of the 'privacy of the home' cannot, it is submitted, be upheld on any substantial grounds of principle (unless, perhaps, by reference to what Professor Gordon has elegantly styled the principle of disfacilitation:[24] to accept the argument, 'I was shipping these films solely for my own use', even when it is true, is to establish too easy a loophole for the commercial distributor of things which it is held undesirable and unlawful to distribute commercially).

How much further can the argument from privacy be pressed as an objection to anti-obscenity laws? That I should be free to peruse what I choose in the privacy of my own room may not avail me much if the choice available in published form is restricted, say, to uplifting works on marxism or religion and on science and mathematics. At this point, the argument should perhaps be viewed in Rawlsian terms as concerning rather the worth of liberty than the existence of liberty; or, rather to re-express his point in directly relevant terms, the worth rather than the recognition of the right of privacy. If we look at the matter first from the point of view of the consumer (so to speak) of literature, painting, photography, drama and all the rest of it, we can with reason say that whatever is a good reason for recognising such a right is *a fortiori* a good reason for maximising its worth. If there are good reasons, as has been contended, for recognising a right of privacy in such matters as those under consideration, there are equally good reasons for extending to the maximum possible range the modes and manners in which, and the subject matters on which, the right may be exercised; for that is to maximise its worth.

One of the practical ways in which the worth of such a right of privacy can be diminished is by restricting the publication of works of whatever kind people may wish to acquire. So from the consumer's point of view the right of privacy, and its underlying value of autonomy, are at least diminished in worth to the extent that the law imposes restrictions on the production and distribution or exhibition of works of whatever kind on grounds of their objectionable content. But what of the producer or distributor? The act of producing or creating any literary or artistic production, however limited in aesthetic merit it may be, is always (or, at the very least, and in dubious cases, may always be claimed to be) an act expressive of the personality of the individual creator. A concern for individual autonomy can be extended to the protection of the rights of the creator here too, as part of or analogous to his basic right of privacy. Private communication or display of such productions among the circle of one's intimates can be no less included within the realm of privacy.

But do these rights extend to cover distribution in an open market? Here, I think, the answer must be negative. The mere fact that an act is an act of a private citizen does not make it a private act. The right to draw or write or take photographs howsoever one wishes to do in private, and the right to communication of one's creation to chosen individuals of one's own acquaintance are both rights which belong within the wider ambit of a right of individual privacy. They are different in substance from an asserted right to address oneself openly and generally to the public at large, or to vend one's productions in an open market to people in general.

To say that freedom of public debate, discussion and display is different from, and raises different issues from, the freedoms entailed by rights to privacy is not to accord them less importance. The right to public speech is indeed no less vital than the right to private thought. But it is different, and it rests upon different considerations, and may be opposed by different countervailing considerations. The problem of public order and disorder is posed here as it it not directly posed by private activities. And here, by parity of reasoning, the question of the legitimacy of the laying down of norms and standards of public decency must be confronted, and (apart from the question of the worth of the consumer's right of privacy) it does not seem possible to set up the right of individual privacy as a directly relevant counter to the claim of public decency, whatever it is worth.

This is neither the time nor the place to pursue that point much further. The arguments in favour of the greatest possible freedom of public speech discussion and debate are too well known to require further rehearsal here. Whether one looks at the matter from the point of view of a general interest in the furtherance by free discussion of truth in all its manifestations, or from the point of view of the individual's freedom and dignity as a participant in the processes of a free society, the setting of limits on freedom of speech and expression must always be subject to the most stringent scrutiny, and there is a formidable onus to be borne in justifying such limits. However, there may still be a greater range of legitimate limitations on public than on private conduct.

For myself, I am far from convinced that prohibitions on publication of material based solely on the ground of their breach or flagration of canons of decency do constitute legitimate limitations (save in so far as particular publications are directly invasive of the rights of determinate individuals, including rights of privacy in the exceptional cases discussed above where they are so invaded). But I would suggest at least this: that such restrictions on public conduct would be at least in some degree less difficult to justify if they were drawn in such a way as to secure a clear protection for genuinely private activities in the sense of activities private to voluntary participants and not obtrusive to the view of those having no wish to join in. If a majority favours the legal maintenance of given canons of public decency, it does not follow automatically that the majority is justified in so doing. But at least one of the obvious objections is met if the majority concedes clear rights of privacy to minorities who do not share or respect the same canons of decency. I strongly doubt whether either the Scots or the English laws on obscenity or obscene publications do achieve any such balance, in the way of a full recognition of rights of privacy in such matters. It seems clear that the current majority of the U.S. Supreme Court does not do so either.

But that is not the issue which this paper set out to consider, and on the issue proposed the argument may now be drawn to a conclusion. Privacy and obscenity are indeed mutually relevant topics, but in a more restricted sense than is sometimes supposed. It is certainly true that recognition of a right of individual privacy is inconsistent with certain forms of restriction on the possession, use or private enjoyment or circulation of materials deemed obscene. Considerations of the worth of such a right tell against the legitimacy of restraints on publication or distribution of such materials, as do other arguments concerning the importance of securing the freedom of public speech and expression by private individuals. But the right of privacy cannot itself be set up in direct opposition to prohibitions on obscene publications or public displays or performances. The drawing of a clear and justified distinction between public and private activity, in so far as it genuinely secures a generously defined right of privacy may indeed remove one common and strong objection to legislation on obscene publications and cognate subjects. Whether there are, and what might be, the positive justifications of such legislation, has not been here considered; but it has been demonstrated that, contrary to a widely and influentially held opinion, obscene publications cannot, save in special and exceptional cases, be attacked on the ground that they themselves are intrusive upon privacy or rights thereto.[25]

NOTES AND REFERENCES

1. 394 U.S. 557; 22 L.Ed. 2d 542.
2. 394 U.S. 568; 22 L.Ed. 2d 551.
3. 394 U.S. 564; 22 L.Ed. 2d 549.
4. 394 U.S. 565; 22 L.Ed. 2d 549–50.
5. 394 U.S. 568 fn. 11; 22 L.Ed. 2d 551 fn. 11.
6. 354 U.S. 476; 1 L.Ed. 2d 1498.
7. ibid, 485; 1507.
8. 394 U.S. 567; 22 L.Ed. 2d 551.
9. 413 U.S. 123; 37 L.Ed. 2d 500 and 413 v.s. 139; 37 L.Ed. 2d 513.
10. 402 U.S. 363; at 376 28 L.Ed. 2d 822.
11. 413 U.S. at 142–4; 37 L.Ed. 2d at 517–19.
12. 413 U.S. 128–9; 37 L.Ed. 2d 506.
13. 413 U.S. 137; 37 L.Ed. 2d 511.
14. 415 U.S. 49; 37 L.Ed. 2d 446.
15. 22 The Public Interest 25–6 (Winter 1971), [Emphasis added by C. J. Burger in citing quoted passage at 413 U.S. 59; 37 L.Ed. 2d 458.]
16. *Pornography: The Longford Report* (London, 1972).

17. D. N. MacCormick 'A Note Upon Privacy', (1973) 89 L.Q.R. 23–7; 'Privacy: a Problem of Definition?' (1974) 1 B.J.L.S. 75–8. But note also N. S. Marsh's rejoinder to the former, at 89 L.Q.R. 183.

18. See Charles Fried *An Anatomy of Values* (1970) 139; also 77 L. J. Yale 1968, 475; and compare P. Stein and J. Shand *Legal Values in Western Society* (Edinburgh, Edinburgh University Press, 1974) Ch. 8, esp. at pp. 192–3.

19. For discussion of the concept, see D. N. MacCormick and J. Raz 'Voluntary Obligations and Normative Powers', in Aristotelian Society Supplementary Volume XLVI (1972) 59–102.

20. For the notion of privacy as involving control, see A. F. West in *Privacy and Freedom* (1967), e.g. at p. 7.

21. Cf. *Report of the Committee on Privacy* 1972 Cmnd. 5012 paras. 98–113.

22. This is indeed an objection to the present argument which has been most forcefully put to me by my colleague Professor Robert S. Summers.

23. See J. Austin *Lectures on Jurisprudence,* lecture 17.

24. G. H. Gordon *The Criminal Law of Scotland* (Edinburgh, W. Green & Son Ltd., 1967) pp. 218–20.

25. For criticism of and advice on drafts of this paper, I am much indebted to Mr. Z. K. Bankowski, Mr. Christie Davies, Dr. R. Dhavan, Mr K. Haakonssen and most of all Professor R. S. Summers, not all of whose points of criticism I have met in full. Naturally the views expressed and any defects in the argument are my sole responsibility.

Film Censorship and the Law

by John Trevelyan

I was responsible for film censorship in Britain from 1958 to 1971, and can write about it with professional experience. I am not a lawyer, so my comments on the law are those of an amateur and not a professional.

Film censorship is the only external censorship of the media of communication and entertainment that survives in Britain. Up to 1968, when Parliament passed the Theatres Act, stage plays were subject to censorship by the Lord Chamberlain; since then they have been free from censorship but subject to the provisions of the law. Television and radio are not censored by any external body, but there is a form of internal censorship, and both the B.B.C. and I.B.A. seem to be sensitive to complaints. Books, newspapers and publications are not subject to external censorship, but are also subject to the provisions of the law.

It may well be asked why censorship of films should survive, especially now that the theatre has been freed. I suggest that the probable answer is that on the whole the present system of film censorship has worked fairly successfully, and that it fulfils an important function in the protection of children, a function that is more relevant to cinema than to theatre. It would also require an Act of Parliament to get rid of it, the fact that, since 1968, the topic of censorship has become more controversial, tends to make politicians rather reluctant to introduce a bill to abolish it.

As a form of control censorship has the advantage that it can be more flexible than law, provided that, as with film censorship in Britain, it operates without written rules or published policy. Its decisions can reflect changes in public attitudes, whereas law is concerned with exact interpretation by the courts of Acts of

Parliament, and can only have some flexibility if juries, in arriving at verdicts, reflect contemporary attitudes, even if judges have directed them otherwise, as not infrequently happens.

Even so, censorship is, and must be, open to the criticism that there is no justification for a few people having the power to decide what films the public may or may not see. Censorship judgments are largely subjective judgments, and this results in decisions being influenced by personal tastes and prejudices. It is sometimes said that all censorship is basically political, and, although I would not entirely agree with this, I would say that censorship can all too easily become political. In most countries where there is film censorship it is a government-controlled operation, and therefore must be political in essence. At least in Britain since the last war there has been no political censorship of films; up to the end of the war there was political censorship, and, surprisingly enough, it was rarely questioned.

The British system of operating film censorship is, I think, unique, and, like some other British institutions, it came into existence without any deliberate design. In the early years of the present century, when the cinema started to become a popular entertainment there was some concern about fire risks. The film stock was highly inflammable and films were being shown in buildings that had not been designed for the purpose. So in 1909 Parliament passed the first Cinematograph Act to deal with this risk. Under this Act all buildings used as cinemas were required to have a licence issued by the local authority, which had to be satisfied that there were adequate fire precautions. The Act was, however, drafted in such a way as to give the authorities wider power of control over what was shown on the screen, thus making the local authorities film censors in law.

The film industry, which had previously suffered from interference by some local authorities, was concerned about this, since it appeared that they might have to submit all their films to all the local authorities for censorship before they could be shown in cinemas, which would be an aggravating and costly business. So they sent a delegation to the Home Secretary and proposed that they should set up an independent censorship board which would view all films and decide on their suitability: they also proposed that the Home Secretary should appoint an official of his Department as an arbiter in cases of appeal. The Home Secretary welcomed the main proposal but not the ancillary proposal, since he was reluctant for himself or his Department to be involved in something that might well be controversial, a view which has been held by all subsequent Home Secretaries.

The British Board of Film Censors was then set up, with a President, Mr. G. A. Redford, who had been Reader of Plays for the Lord Chamberlain, and a small number of examiners, and started its work on 1 January 1913. In its early years there were problems. The film industry was, on the whole, co-operative and sent in films for censorship, but some local authorities were less co-operative and continued to act as independent bodies of censors. In 1915 the President of the Board and representatives of the film industry approached the Home Secretary and said that in their opinion the Board should become an official censorship body under his responsibility. The Home Secretary said that it would be necessary for him to consult the local authorities, who had the legal powers, before reaching a decision, and this resulted in delay. At this stage there were important changes: there was a change of Home Secretary and Mr. Redford, first President of the Board, died. He was replaced by an outstanding personality, Mr. T. P. O'Connor, M.P., an experienced journalist, who succeeded in a short time in gaining the confidence of the government, the local authorities and the film industry: but for him we would have had government-controlled, and therefore political, censorship.

Instead of this we had a gradual development of the present system, under which all films to be shown in commercial cinemas are first censored by the British Board of Film Censors, which is still an independent organisation. But any local authority licensing cinemas is legally entitled to reverse or modify any decision that the Board makes on films to be shown in cinemas under its control. In practice the decisions of the Board are almost always accepted by local authorities, but they do act from time to time as appeal bodies, and sometimes take up individual complaints, so there is some degree of variation. One Home Secretary, Herbert Morrison, who, in retirement, became President of the Board, said in the House of Commons in 1942:

> I freely admit that this is a curious arrangement, but the British have a very great habit of making curious arrangements work very well, and this works. Frankly, I do not wish to be the Minister who has to answer questions in the House as to whether particular films should or should not

be censored. I think it would be dangerous for the Home Secretary to have direct powers himself in the matter.

From time to time since then there have been further statements in the House from Home Secretaries expressing satisfaction with the present system.

This, then, is the background to film censorship in Britain. For sixty years the British Board of Film Censors has been a protection to the film industry, a protection from unreasonable interference by the local authorities and a protection for the film industry from court proceedings. But recently the situation has changed.

During my time at the Board we were pursuing a policy of progressive liberalisation, essentially when dealing with films showing sex, while retaining a rather stricter control over films showing violence, although accepting violence when it was used 'for a good reason'. This policy seemed to meet with general approval. We were aware of changing public attitudes, and reflected this in our decisions. At about the time of my retirement, in 1971, we became aware of an organised 'backlash'. Something of the same kind had been experienced in the United States, partially as a result of a spread of pornography, so it was not entirely unexpected here. The old traditions of morality were being threatened, and this produced a reaction, not from the many but from the vociferous few. In 1971 and 1972 objections were raised to certain films, notably *The Devils, Straw Dogs* and *A Clockwork Orange*, and organised pressure came from the Festival of Light. Publicity was given to these objections, and this ensured the commercial success of the films that were attacked. In 1973 the target was *Last Tango in Paris*, and in 1974 *The Exorcist*; the public flocked to see them.

Presumably as a result of this, recourse was had to the law, and in 1974 proceedings were taken as a result of the exhibition of two films. First, as a result of a single complaint, proceedings were taken against United Artists Film Corporation for distributing an obscene film, *Last Tango in Paris*, which had been passed by the Board and had been shown in a London cinema for a considerable time without complaint; secondly the police, acting on a single complaint apparently with the approval of the Director of Public Prosecutions, seized from a London cinema a Swedish sex-education film, *More of the Language of Love*, which, although not passed by the Board, had been passed for exhibition by the Greater London Council.

In the case against United Artists charges were made under the Obscene Publications Act of 1959. Up to this time it had been accepted that this Act specifically excluded films, since they were covered by the Cinematograph Acts of 1909 and 1952, and indeed this argument was put forward in a lower court. But at a later stage the Lord Chief Justice ruled that proceedings under this Act against a distributor were valid, although agreeing that this point of legal validity could remain open for further judgment when the trial was held.

Under the Obscene Publications Act it is an offence to publish an obscene article for gain, and Section 1 (3) of the Act defines 'publication' as follows:

> For the purposes of this Act a person publishes an article who (a) distributes, circulates, sells, lets on hire, gives, or lends it, or who offers it for sale or for letting on hire; or (b) in the case of an article containing or embodying matter to be looked at, or a record, shows, plays or projects it.

This is, however, followed by a proviso which reads as follows:

> Provided that paragraph (b) of this section shall not apply to anything done in the course of a cinematographic exhibition (within the meaning of the Cinematograph Act 1952) other than one excluded from the Cinematograph Act 1909, by subsection (4) of Section 7 of that Act (which relates to exhibitions in private houses to which the public are not admitted), or to anything done in the course of television or sound broadcasting.

It was held by the Lord Chief Justice that a film distributor was open to proceedings under Section 1 (3) paragraph (a), and that since this was not under paragraph (b) the proviso did not apply.

However, the trial judge thought otherwise and ruled that the proceedings were legally invalid, so the charges were dismissed. Then, in view of the conflicting legal opinions, the Attorney General submitted the matter to the Court of Appeal, taking the unusual course of supporting the decision of the trial judge. The Court of Appeal concurred with the trial judge's decision on the facts of this particular case, but in the judgment implied that there might be other cases on which the decision, based on the facts of the case, would be different.

The second case was also important. This was a private prosecution, under Common Law, of the owners and managers of a London cinema for conspiring to show an indecent film, *More of the Language of Love,* under a licence issued by the Greater London

Council. In this case the prosecution was successful, and the defendants were duly fined.

Encouraged by this success, in 1975 the same person initiated charges under Common Law relating to an earlier sex-education film, *The Language of Love*. This film had originally been refused a certificate by the Board, but had subsequently been passed for exhibition by the Greater London Council and by more than one hundred licensing authorities, and had been seen, without complaint, by one and a half million people, so that eventually the Board reversed its earlier decision and passed the film for exhibition to adults. Charges were laid against the President and Secretary of the Board and against the film exhibitors. The court dismissed the charges against the officers of the Board, but not those against the film exhibitors, which were referred to a higher court. At the subsequent hearing these charges were also dismissed with costs.

At this time the Law Commission were considering Common Law, and subsequently recommended that its use for such charges should be discontinued. This recommendation has not yet been adopted. The Director of Public Prosecutions may now make further use of the Obscene Publications Acts since the Court of Appeal has ruled against the admissibility of expert evidence testifying to therapeutic benefit to sexual deviants, thus limiting expert evidence to literary quality, artistic quality or educational value.

We now therefore have the position that censorship, either by the Board or by a local authority, provides no certain protection for a film distributor or film exhibitor. Furthermore, as a result of recent court proceedings, it now appears that film producers, film directors, camera operators and actors can find themselves in the courts for taking part in the making of obscene films, and, if convicted, can find themselves in prison.

This is a matter for concern. The basic problem of the obscenity laws is that there is no exact legal definition of 'obscenity', or, in Common Law charges of 'indecency'. It therefore becomes a matter of opinion, and verdicts depend entirely on the subjective judgments of members of juries, who may possibly be influenced by the subjective opinions and prejudices of judges. The defence can have some say, if not much, in the selection of juries, but has no say in the selection of judges.

Perhaps not surprisingly, judges tend not to reflect contemporary attitudes. They tend to be older men, and to mix with their own generation rather than with younger people. They represent 'The Establishment', and tend to be less than sympathetic to people who want changes in society; an outstanding example of this was in the *Oz* case, in which the obscenity laws seemed to be used for a political purpose; the judge left no doubt about his personal views on what the defendants represented. The report of the Working Party of the Arts Council of Great Britain, published in 1969, summarised the position as follows:

> The present situation is that judge, jury, witnesses, prosecution and defendant are all operating in limbo with no meaningful statute to help them, and are themselves condemned to the use of words and phrases that beg whatever question may be the unrevealed purpose of the trial.

This is, without question, a deplorable position.

It appears that in dealing with films the law is concerned only with obscenity, but, as I have already said, it has so far not been able to provide any exact definition of obscenity. The nearest definition, which was made in the Hicklin judgment of 1868, is as follows:

> . . . an article shall be deemed to be obscene if its effect or (where the article comprises two or more distinct items) the effect of any one of its items is, if taken as a whole, such as to tend to deprave and corrupt persons who are likely, having regard to all relevant circumstances, to read, see or hear the matter contained or embodied in it.

This requires a definition of the words 'deprave' and 'corrupt' and in this the standard dictionaries are of little help since each of these words is used as a definition of the other.

It is, however, obvious that in the eyes of the law obscenity is solely concerned with sex. Some of us find violence, sadism, war, poverty and starvation more obscene than sex, but the law does not recognise this. The law reflects the sexual inhibitions of our own society, in turn a long-term reaction to the 'permissiveness' of the Restoration and the reign of George IV.

About ten years ago there was an important argument between Lord Devlin and Professor H. L. A. Hart, on the law and morality, which is set out in detail in their respective books – *The Enforcement of Morals* by Patrick Devlin and *Law, Liberty and Morality* by H. L. A. Hart. These books contain the core of one problem – is it, or is it not, for the law to maintain standards of morality in our society? Lord Devlin writes:

. . . the true principle is that the law exists for the protection of society. It does not discharge its function by protecting the individual from injury, annoyance, corruption and exploitation; the law must protect also the institutions and the community of ideas, political and moral, without which people cannot live together. Society cannot ignore the morality of the individual any more than it can his loyalty; it flourishes on both and without either it dies.

In a legal judgment ten years earlier, when the book *The Image and the Search* was prosecuted, he said:

Just as loyalty is one of the things which is essential to the well-being of a nation, so some sense of morality is something that is essential to the well-being of a nation, and the healthy life of a community, and, accordingly, anyone who seeks by his writing to corrupt that fundamental sense of morality is guilty of obscene libel . . . If there is a conflict in an artist or a writer between his desire for self-expression and the sense that morality is fundamental to the well-being of the community (if there is such a conflict), then it is morality that must prevail.

Hart, in his reply, quotes the Wolfenden Report – 'There must remain a realm of private morality which is, in brief and crude terms, not the law's business', and John Stuart Mill, who in his great essay 'On Liberty' wrote:

The only purpose for which power can rightfully be exercised over any member of a civilised community against his will is to prevent harm to others . . . His own good, either physical or moral, is not a sufficient warrant. He cannot rightfully be compelled to do or forbear because it will make him happier, because in the opinion of others to do so would be wise or even right.

Being on the side of Hart and Mill, I would add another quotation from Mill's essay:

The only freedom which deserves the name is that of pursuing our own good in our own way, so long as we do not attempt to deprive others of theirs or impede their efforts to obtain it. Each is the proper guardian of his own health, whether bodily or mental and spiritual. Mankind are greater gainers by suffering each other to live as seems good to themselves than by compelling each to live as seems good to the rest.

This is the core of the problem about film censorship and the law. Accepting that children, and perhaps young people, need protection, do we need the law or censorship to protect the adult? I do not think so. I think it is time that we not only allowed, but encouraged, the adult to grow up and to choose for himself what he wants to do, what films he wants to see, what he wants to read, provided that in so doing he does no harm to other people; if he does harm to himself that is no concern of law or censorship.

What then would I recommend? First, I would want film censorship to continue on much the same lines as at present, certainly with an independent censorship board, but to confine its activities to the protection of children and young people. Films that are not considered suitable for the young should be given an 'X' Certificate without cuts or reservations of any kind, anyone of eighteen years or more should be legally free to see any film, but there should be stronger penalties than there are now if young people under this age are admitted, and a more effective enforcement.

Secondly, I would want careful consideration to be given to the repeal of the obscenity laws. The Working Party set up by the Arts Council of Great Britain considered amending legislation, but eventually rejected it because they could produce no exact definition of 'obscenity' and believed that without this there could be no guarantee of justice. They therefore recommended repeal of the obscenity laws. At much the same time a Commission appointed by the President of the United States to consider the spread of obscenity and pornography made exactly similar recommendations. In neither country have these recommendations yet been adopted. In each country fortunes are being made because restrictive legislation has provided an attraction for sexual material that any well-adjusted adult would find puerile.

Before recommending repeal of the obscenity laws I would put them to one further test. I would like to see the appointment of a committee of expert lawyers entrusted with the task of seeing whether it is possible to draft a sensible and workable Act of Parliament which could contain exact definitions of what should be prohibited. My reason for this recommendation is that I believe this to be impossible, and that until it has been proved to be impossible it will be difficult to get Parliament to agree to repeal, which should be the ultimate aim.

There are, however, certain things that I would like to see prohibited by law, even in the sexual field. I would want to prohibit the use of children for the production of pornography, or for anything of this kind, and, out of kindness to animals, I would include them too. I would like to control other kinds of obscenity, such as I referred to earlier, not by censorship or law, but by creating a world which would not tolerate violence, sadism, war, poverty and starvation in any country. Sex, even if pornographic or obscene, cannot harm human beings as much as any of these, and can make people happy.

I believe that human beings cannot be happy unless they have freedom, particularly freedom from want and from fear, but also freedom to be themselves, to choose for themselves, always, however, with the proviso that in their choice and actions they are not harming other people. Restriction by law, or even by censorship, can be harmful by preventing people from developing or growing up, and by not encouraging them to take personal responsibility for what they do. The only justifiable kind of censorship is self-censorship, and we shall never get enough of this if we continue to protect people from things that would be unlikely to harm them and that most well-adjusted people are perfectly well able to cope with.

I leave the last word to John Stuart Mill, who, although writing more than a hundred years ago, wrote what is at least as true and pertinent now as it was then. He ended his essay 'On Liberty' with these words:

> A government cannot have too much of the kind of activity which does not impede, but aids and stimulates individual exertion and development. The mischief begins when instead of calling for the activity and power of individuals and bodies, it substitutes its own activity for theirs; when instead of informing, advising, and upon occasion denouncing, it makes them work in fetters, or bids them stand aside and does their work instead of them. The worth of a State, in the long run, is the worth of the individuals composing it; and a State which postpones the interests of their mental expansion and elevation to a little more of administrative skill, or that semblance of it which practice gives in the details of business; a State which dwarfs its men in order that they may be more docile instruments in its hands, even for beneficial purposes, will find that with small men no great thing can be accomplished; and that the perfection of machinery to which it has sacrificed everything will in the end avail it nothing for want of the vital power which, in order that the machine might work more smoothly, it has preferred to banish.

NOTES AND REFERENCES

1. Acts of Parliament: The Cinematograph Act, 1909 (9 Edw. 7 Ch. 30); The Cinematograph Act, 1952 (15 and 16 Geo. 6 and 1 Eliz. 2 Ch. 68); The Obscene Publications Act, 1959 (7 and 8 Eliz. 2 Ch. 66); The Obscene Publications Act 1964 (12 and 13 Eliz. 2 Ch. 74); The Theatres Act 1968 (16 and 17 Eliz. 2 Ch. 54).

2. *Report of the Committee on Homosexual Offences and Prostitution* (1957) Cmnd. 247.
3. *Report of the Joint Committee on Censorship of the Theatre* (1967) Cmnd.
4. Neville March Hummings: *Film Censors and the Law,* London, George Allen & Unwin (1967).
5. Patrick Devlin: *The Enforcement of Morals,* Oxford University Press (1965).
6. H. L. A. Hart: *Law, Liberty and Morality,* Oxford University Press (1963).
7. Arts Council of Great Britain: *The Obscenity Laws – A Report by a Working Party set up at a Conference convened by the Chairman of the Arts Council of Great Britain,* London, Andre Deutsch (1969).
8. C. H. Rolph (ed.): *The Trial of Lady Chatterley,* London, Penguin Books (1961).
9. T. Palmer: *The Trials of Oz,* London, Blond and Briggs (1971).
10. *The Report of the Commission on Obscenity and Pornography,* New York, Bantam Books (1970).
11. *Pornography: The Longford Report,* London, Coronet Books (1972).
12. John Trevelyan: *What the Censor Saw,* London, Michael Joseph (1973).
13. Guy Phelps: *Film Censorship,* London, Gollancz (1975).
14. J. S. Mill: *On Liberty* (1859 – reprinted in the World's Classics series).

SECTION III

What are the Effects of Censoring or not Censoring Obscenity?

Pornography in Denmark – a General Survey

by Berl Kutchinsky

Pornography is an example of a rather trifling issue which – due to certain constellations of forces at a certain juncture in the cultural history of the Western World has become a major issue of the day. Though of ephemeral importance it has, in most countries, precipitated heated debate in public and in private, in the mass media and in literature, in parliament and in the courts, in committees and in commissions.

The 'porno wave' – a metaphor referring both to the period in which pornography has become easily available and widely distributed, and to the period in which the topic of pornography has become 'an issue' – varies in depth and intensity from one country to another. In Denmark it began around 1964 and had receded by 1970. In countries like Great Britain and the U.S.A., the controversies and the porno wave have lingered on. One major reason is active opposition to the availability of pornography. The more active the opposition against pornography – the longer pornography remains an issue. Inevitably it will be longer before the point of general satisfaction and satiation is reached. *If* pornography is a vile monster – another metaphor sometimes used about this material by its most vehement opponents – it belongs to the special breed of science-fiction monsters which are nourished by the explosives being shot at it. This kind of monster – assuming it is one – starves and withers through lack of attention. After all, a monster only remains ominous as long as it is able to scare people.

Is pornography a monster? In Denmark it has been in abundant supply for a long time. Since 1969 it has even been free from the legal restraints which exist in most other countries. The Danish experience tells us that pornography is not a subject to be scared of. In this paper I shall briefly review the Danish experience. What is pornography like? Who makes it? Who uses it? What do they use it for? Finally, what kind of psychological and social effects does it have ? These questions will be answered on the basis of my own research carried out since 1969 and more fully documented in Kutchinsky (in press) among other publications.

The Danish Porno Wave

Explicit erotic descriptions in pictures as well as in words have existed since antiquity and have flourished at various periods in the cultural histories of Europe and Asia. In the eighteenth and nineteenth centuries Europe experienced a porno wave which as far as number of publications are concerned far surpasses similar porno waves of the present time. It is no accident that the best selling pornographic book in the Danish porno wave, *Fanny Hill,* was written during that period.

Nevertheless, there are at least two distinguishing and unique points about the present situation. Firstly, pornography is becoming the property of the masses while earlier it was more or less restricted to the economic and intellectual upper class. In Denmark this is already the case. Secondly, pornography is about to become morally and socially acceptable and even legal, which has not been the case for at least the past 400 years (Alschuler, 1971).

This brief paper cannot fully analyse the reasons for this development. But let me point out what I consider to be decisive factors. The first factor is that new technologies have made possible the mass production of colour magazines and films of high technical quality at a very low cost. The second – and no doubt the most important factor – has been the emergence of a more liberalised view of sexual behaviour, which has exonerated the naked body and the sexual act from certain indictments of sinfulness. This new sexual liberalism, the so-called 'sexual revolution', has been influential in several different ways. It has awakened and strengthened a latent need for erotica among many people. It has made possible the economic exploitation of this new attitude. And it paved the way for a more lenient enforcement and perhaps eventual abolition of existing bans. This development emerged through an accelerated interaction between three groups: the producer, the consumer and the authorities – with the mass-media playing the hard-working and indispensable intermediary role.

In Denmark it is possible to distinguish two distinct phases of the contemporary pornography era. 'The literary porno wave' first began around 1962. Compare the printing figures of the last two years, a total of 75,000 copies of erotic books, with the figures for 1962 alone, almost a quarter of a million copies, to which should be added about 200,000 copies of sexual education books. During the subsequent years the production of erotic books increased steadily until 1965, when *Fanny Hill* was acquitted by the Supreme Court (Waaben, in press) creating an almost free market for pornographic literature. This resulted in a further steep increase, until the production reached its climax with 1.4 million copies in 1967. This was the year in which the legal ban on pornographic literature was repealed. By 1969 the era of porno literature was completely over.

During the period 1962–8 Danish publishers printed more than 5.3 million erotic books, which averages out at about 1.2 copies per inhabitant. It is therefore no wonder that most Danes acquainted themselves with porno literature during these years. This was confirmed in a study in which a representative sample from the Copenhagen adult population, 400 men and women aged eighteen to sixty years, were interviewed about their use of pornography. No less than 87% of the men and 70% of the women had read at least one pornographic book. However, there were great differences as to how many books people had read. While 12% of the men interviewed had not read more than a single book, 8% had read more than 50 books. The female subjects had read about half as much as the males. But here too there were great individual differences and while 27% had not read any porno books at all, 20% had read ten books or more.

Literary pornography dominated the scene in Denmark until the mid-1960s, while descriptions acceptable in words were not yet tolerable in pictures. Then followed an influx of the so-called 'porno-magazines'. Until 1965, there were numerous 'girlie' or 'nude' magazines depicting near-naked pin-ups or sun bathers. However, later magazines began to depict pubic hair, and models were shown spreading their legs and showing their genitalia. A significant change in picture pornography occurred when the first so-called 'petting' magazines showed two or more models together in erotic, but non-coital situations. At the same time, pin-up girls became overtly provocative. The sale of these magazines quickly reached millions, in spite of – or perhaps rather because of – numerous police crack-downs and seizures.

The 'petting' magazines did not dare show active sexual organs. The first coital pictures existed only in the form of black-and-white photo series. But from 1967 the production of actual (illegal) porno magazines began. The first ones were black-and-white coital pictures with single couples. During the years 1968–9 these developed into full-colour magazines with group sex in all thinkable variations. Some, though few, homosexual and sado-masochistic magazines were also produced, but these, until quite recently, were of very poor technical quality. Since 1970 a number of variations and specialities have appeared: women who have intercourse with animals (dogs, horses, hogs, etc.), pictures including children, and the so-called 'bizarre' magazines, showing persons urinating or defecating. Among the ordinary colour picture magazines (in which hetero-sexual 'normal' group sex still strongly dominates) there are a number of Swedish and Danish magazines with both text and pictures. The Swedish magazines emphasise good technical quality and layout; the Danish ones (the most well known being *Week-End Sex*) have a cheaper style and slightly sadistic touch. Recently some ordinary porno picture magazines have begun to print pornographic short stories, the text being usually only in English and German.

The sale of pornographic magazines is more difficult to estimate than that of books. It is quite certain, however, that since 1965 more than one million copies of such magazines have been sold to the Danes per year. Sales increased steadily to two or three million magazines by 1969, but since then the consumption of pornography by the Danish reader has considerably decreased. This decrease has reduced the output of the publishers very little; they have been compensated by an increasing export market. But it is important to note that even when the picture porno wave was at its climax, the sale of pornographic magazines made up only a very small part of the total volume of entertainment magazines sold, men's and women's weeklies, hobby journals, comics, etc.; the latter, in 1969, amounted to about 130 million copies.

The study of adult Copenhageners mentioned earlier, showed that in December 1969, 88% of the men and 73% of the women had seen at least one pornographic picture magazine. No less than 39% of the men and 23% of the women had read one during the previous month. On average, males had read approximately three times as many magazines as the women. 15% of the men had seen an average of 150 to 170 magazines altogether, while 12% had not seen any magazines at all. Among the women, about 10% had read an average of 75 magazines, while 27% had not seen any at all.

Pornographic films account for a good part of the total turnover in the porno business. Nevertheless, only a few of the subjects in the Copenhagen investigation of 1969 had ever seen a pornographic film. Undoubtedly this situation has now changed, for since 1970 pornographic films have been shown in public cinemas all over Denmark.

WHAT IS PORNOGRAPHY USED FOR?

We have shown that a majority of Copenhageners became acquainted with pornography during the years of the porno wave. This is probably true now of the majority of adult Danes outside Copenhagen. This does not mean there is an obsession with pornography in Denmark. It merely reflects the fact that por- nography has become a generally accessible commodity. It is almost as easy to get hold of as comic magazines or women's weeklies. The extreme porno wave, i.e. the fact that production and sales output reached considerable heights in the course of a very few years, is wholly due to the fact that such sale had hitherto been forbidden. The interest in pornography during the second part of the sixties was, above all, an expression of curiosity. Everybody wanted to know what this much debated matter was about. There is a resemblance between this development and what could be observed after the Second World War when the first much-longed-for banana boats came to Denmark. Bananas hit the front pages, everybody talked about and ate bananas until a satiation point was reached. Today there are quite a few people who rarely or never eat bananas. A few people eat a lot of bananas; most people enjoy bananas once in a while. This development is a kind of reaction which I have elsewhere called 'The Banana Boat Effect' (Kutchinsky, 1973a).

So the answer to the question, 'What has the enormous amount of pornography sold during the porno wave been used for?' is that it was used to satisfy a temporary curiosity. Apart from this, however, our investigations show that pornography is mainly used for two purposes: for entertainment and to accompany masturbation or, more rarely, coitus.

The use of pornography as a means of sexual arousal or aphrodisiac emerges from the answers to some of the questions in the study mentioned earlier. It was found, first of all, that 48% of the men and 29% of the women thought that either pornographic books, pictures or films could be sexually arousing. 14% of both men and women found books exciting. Twice as many men as women, 22% as against 11%, found pictures arousing. Three times as many men as women, 16% as against 5%, thought that pornographic films were sexually arousing.

20% of the men and 5% of the women in the study said that they sometimes use pornography when masturbating. 6% of the men and 10% of the women said that they used pornography once in a while in association with sexual intercourse. Although the sample was small it is interesting to note that twice as many women used pornography in association with intercourse as with masturbation.

WHO ARE THE PORNO USERS?

As already stated, the amount of pornography used, whether books or picture magazines, is considerably larger among men than among women. There are also more men than women who find pornography arousing and who use it for masturbation. Nevertheless, the difference between males and females in this respect is considerably less than was found in earlier studies of this type. About thirty years ago Kinsey (1953, p. 672) found that porno users in the U.S.A. were almost exclusively males. However, recent American studies, carried out or ordered by the U.S. Commission on Obscenity and Pornography, have arrived at the same conclusions as we have. From this one can assume that in recent years there has been a considerable increase in women's interest in the use of pornography. This change doubtless has something to do with the increased acceptance, by both sexes, that women are interested in these matters. A parallel can perhaps be seen in a change in the 'public' attitudes towards female masturbation.

The remaining difference between men's and women's interest in and use of pornography may be explained by the fact that the type of pornography produced so far caters mainly for the male appetite. It is arguable, as Kinsey thought, that there is also a biological explanation in that males are more likely to be sexually stimulated by pornography (especially by pictorial pornography) than women. Whether this is true or not, there is hardly any doubt that the somewhat callous and unromantic intense preoccupation with the sexual organs and sexual act is a masculine characteristic in our culture. It is possible that the feminine equivalent of the elaborate porno magazines of the males are the 'true romance' magazines. Since that kind of popular literature is still very much alive, the increased interest of women in sexual matters which have hitherto been considered rather exclusively masculine can perhaps be understood as part of a general extension, rather than a change, in women's patterns of sexual attitudes and behaviour.

Another important background variable is age. Young people are generally more interested in pornography than are older people; this is true of both men and women. Young men use pornography for masturbation more often than older men; among women there is a tendency in the opposite direction. A more permanent interest in and frequent use of pornography is found among males aged between twenty-five and forty. This coincides with the results of a study of Copenhagen porno shop customers, who belong primarily to that age group.

As might be expected, therefore, gender and age were the more important background variables. It is surprising however, that no particular connection could be established between the use of pornography and social or educational level. Kinsey's investigations, as well as the new American studies, have shown that more pornography was consumed by the better educated or higher social classes. The Danish experience suggests that this difference disappears when pornography becomes more available. In other words, people from the lower social strata, with a lower educational standard are probably just as interested, or uninterested, in pornography as everybody else. But if pornography is difficult to obtain and therefore expensive, then it is obtained primarily by those with money and connections.

Equally surprising but more difficult to explain was the fact that religious and political conviction could not be closely correlated with the use of pornography.

While gender and age were influential factors as to whether a particular person would be interested in pornography, the real determining elements were of course individual psychological and social factors. Analysis of the information available so far suggests that, providing pornography is easily available, the individual consumption of this material is primarily dependent on two factors: (1) the general strength of the sexual drive and (2) the degree to which this drive can be satisfied in a social context. With some modification, these criteria could probably also be applied to the frequency of masturbation. There is little doubt that masturbation and the use of pornography are closely related. It is evident too that the need for pornography is greater for those whose sexual satisfaction is exclusively dependent upon masturbation, the 'sexually lonely', than for those whose masturbation is an addition to an active, social, sex life.

A regular and extensive use of pornography is therefore found primarily among persons who have a strong sexual drive and who, for some reason or another, suffer from a degree of 'sociosexual deficit'. Obviously, so-called 'sexual deviants' are likely to be sexually lonely more often than non-deviants, and are, all other things being equal, more likely to become regular and extensive users of pornography. The important point here is that sexual deviants become users of pornography not because they are sexually deviant, but because their sexual deviance makes them sexually lonely. In other words, our experience indicates that the use of pornography, even when extensive and frequent, is a normal reaction to what may sometimes be abnormal conditions of life.

Another group of relatively large-scale consumers of pornography have a strong sexual drive but do not appear to be sociosexually deprived – quite the opposite! To these persons an interest in pornography is merely part of a strong and varied interest in sexual matters and activities. The total consumption of pornography in this category may be large, but the use does not have the regularity of the above-mentioned group of sociosexually deprived people.

THE EFFECTS OF PORNOGRAPHY

Recently considerable interest has been expressed in the psychological and social effects of pornography. This interest is justified for many reasons. In the past hundreds of thousands of works of literature – valuable and valueless alike – have been destroyed. Publishers, printers and booksellers have been punished severely for handling them because it was thought that erotic books could have serious damaging effects on their readers. In most parts of the world today, both secular and religious authorities still believe that pornography attacks morality, produces sexual perversions and sexual offences and causes psychological and social imbalance and disruption.

Opinions about the harmfulness of pornography appear to be closely related to moral attitudes towards pornography. Persons and organisations who consider the depiction of the naked body, sexual organs and the sexual act abominable in itself, usually consider pornography dangerous, both for the public and the individual. Not so long ago, serious medical works would list virtually hundreds of diseases and other ill-effects which could arise from masturbation. Medical scientific progress has helped to eliminate some of these myths but their influence should not be overestimated. The idea that masturbation is dangerous began to disappear when it ceased to be considered sinful. Similarly, the myths about the danger of por-nography tend to disappear – with or without hard scientific evidence – when pornography is no longer considered immoral. And the myth of the danger of pornography will persist – in spite of scientific evidence – for as long as this material is condemned on moral grounds.

The reception of the Danish and American 'obscenity reports' by their respective governments and legislative bodies clearly illustrates my point. In 1966 the permanent Danish Penal Law Commission (consisting of four legal scholars) published a pornography report of 103 pages, including an appendix of opinions from various experts and bodies. The U.S. Commission on Obscenity and Pornography had nineteen members, employed a full time staff of eleven socio-logists, psychologists and lawyers, sponsored and financed scores of scientific investigations and in 1970–1 published a report almost 4000 printed pages long. The Danish report was based on a modest amount of scientific evidence available at the time of its writing. The U.S. report presented and utilised an overwhelming amount of scientific evidence. The two reports arrived at the very same conclusions, namely that there is 'no evidence that exposure to or use of explicit sexual materials play a significant role in the causation of social or individual harms such as crime, delinquency, sexual or nonsexual deviancy or severe emotional disturbances' (*The Report of the Commission on Obscenity and Pornography,* 1970, p. 52). The fates of these two reports in their homelands are well known: The Danish pornography report was favourably received and accepted – in fact a majority of members of all political parties in Parliament voted for the bill recommended by the report. In the U.S.A., the U.S. obscenity report was promptly rejected by the President, and as late as 1973, the U.S. Supreme Court overruled the conclusion of the Commission when deciding that the question of whether there is a direct causal connection between obscenity and anti-social conduct is 'inherently unprovable'.

With blatant frankness and naivety the New York newspaper *Daily News* made its position clear when commenting on some early rumours about the U.S. Commission's findings:

> Our hunch is that this much-touted committee is about to come out with a virtual whitewash of the obscene publications, films and stage plays which are flooding the nation. If that hunch pans out, the $2 million spent on this research obviously will have been a near-criminal waste (*Daily News*, August 6, 1970, p. 47).

The British Longford Report of 1972, is another example of the way in which scientific evidence is either ignored or manipulated to suit the purposes of a morally determined point of view.

If research in these areas has a limited impact that does not mean it is useless. It must be taken seriously by anyone who feels that this must be a 'main principle for penal legislation that criminalisation should not take place merely to support a certain moral conviction' and that 'criminalisation must be based on the assumption that it serves one or several purposes of utility, especially by preventing actions that are fit to harm society as a whole, groups of the population or individual persons' (Danish Commission Report, 1966, p. 48). In short, to anyone who believes that 'it is exceedingly unwise for government to attempt to legislate individual moral values and standards independent of behaviour' (U.S. Commission Report, 1970, p. 55), the scientific evidence of the alleged detrimental effects of pornography assumes crucial importance. For people who adhere to Mill's view on legislation, it is not necessary to *prove* that pornography is *not* dangerous; the mere fact that its dangers have not been established despite several attempts is sufficient to warrant decriminalisation.

There follows a brief account of the results of a number of investigations into the effects of pornography – here the Danish experience is supplemented by some American studies. We look first at the immediate effects and then at the longer-term effects.

The immediate effects of pornography, that is the way people react when they read or view pornography, can be illustrated by an experiment carried out in Copenhagen in 1970. The subjects, seventy-two students of both sexes, mainly married couples, were exposed for one hour to hard-core pornography in the form of films, magazines and reading aloud. Before and after the exposure they filled in questionnaires about their backgrounds and attitudes in various ways. They were asked in various ways to indicate what they felt, sexually as well as otherwise, during the stimulation period.

The results showed *inter alia* that 86% of the men and 61% of the women felt that they had experienced 'genital sensations' at least once during the performance. However, only one-fifth of the men said they had had full erection. Although a majority had reacted sexually at one time or another, sexual feelings did not dominate. Only one-quarter of the experimental subjects (men and women alike) indicated that towards the end of the session they had felt 'sexual arousal' and 'urge for sexual activity'. On the other hand, no less than two-thirds had felt bored and many had felt 'over-satiated' and 'disappointed'. A similar overwhelming boredom was found in the vast majority of the visitors at the Sex Fair in Copenhagen in October 1969.

The conclusion, which is in close agreement with that of other similar investigations, is that when confronted with pornography, most people get certain vague sexual sensations, but most people also quickly tire of it. A minority are sexually aroused to a higher degree. Extremely few express strong feelings of disgust or embarrassment. The investigation also showed that people who are favourably disposed towards pornography from the outset are more likely to react positively, while people who are unfavourably disposed usually react negatively. The experiment summarised here used only students as subjects. Later Danish investigations using non-students as subjects suggest that the findings in the experiments could be generalised to include adult subjects of any educational level. There is no scientific evidence available about the reactions of children to pornography.

The after-effects of pornography can be categorised in various ways. First, we may distinguish between the short-term effects and the long-term effects; secondly, we may distinguish between the effects on ordinary people and the effects on especially predisposed, abnormal individuals. A number of other distinctions will eventually appear.

For good reasons, the short-term effects on 'ordinary people' are the ones which have been most thoroughly investigated. In the Danish experiment it appeared that 13% of the experimental subjects (both men and women) reported an increase in the frequency of their masturbation within twenty-four hours after the pornography performance. Almost twice as many (24%) declared that they had increased the amount of their coital activity within the same period. Thus sexual behaviour in the majority of subjects was unaffected by the pornographic performance.

Whether or not a person increased his or her sexual activity after the pornography performance seemed to be closely correlated with the immediate reactions of that person to the pornography. Those who disliked the pornography or who had quickly become bored by it, or who had otherwise reacted unfavourably to it only responded sexually afterwards in a few rare cases. This connection was particularly close as far as the women were concerned. With great accuracy, one could predict a female subject's sexual response within twenty-four hours on the basis of her immediate reaction to the pornography. Half of the men who had reacted positively to the pornography during the performance increased their sexual activity within twenty-four hours after. It was noticed also that the pornography had practically no sexual after-effects on those men whose sexual life, according to their own estimate, was not very satisfactory. Among the men who indicated that their sexual life was highly satisfactory, coital activity increased in about half (among the women there was no such correlation).

Four days after the porno stimulation, very few experimental subjects thought that their sexual activity had increased, and two weeks afterwards no effects could be traced. The pornography did not influence the sexual behaviour of the participants in any other way (with the exception of one male subject who mentioned that the experiment had inspired him to try a new coital position).

Attempts were also made to study the after-effects of the pornography on the participants' attitudes towards various other matters. Among the results it may be noted that the pornography had no effect on attitudes towards sexual offences. Nor was there any indication that moral attitudes were influenced by the pornography. However the experiment did indicate two clear after-effects. The first was that a large number of participants had become 'sick and tired of pornography'. One hour wallowing in pornography seemed to have satiated their own interest in this material for a long time. Only one man said that the experiment had increased his interest in pornography. The second strong after-effect of the experiment came as a surprise. Part of the questionnaire, which was completed before the porno session and again four days and then two weeks after it, dealt with the participants' interest in trying a number of 'advanced' or 'special' forms of sexual behaviour such as group sex, the use of various sexual implements, sado-masochism, etc. It appeared in a majority of participants that they felt a decreasing interest in such activities – only a few had actually tried them. Whether this was because the pornography dampened a real desire to 'freak out' sexually, or whether the participants had, in expectation of the stimulation period, worked up especially 'liberal' interests, could only be known through further experiments.

It must be concluded that neither the Danish nor the many foreign experiments on the short-term effects of pornography have yielded any support for the supposition that pornography leads to 'moral decay', 'sexual excesses' or 'pornomania'. Two American experiments in which the effects of repeated pornography stimulation were studied over a somewhat longer period yielded the same results. Mann, Sidman & Starr (1971, 1973) used eighty-five middle-aged married couples as subjects in an experiment on the effects of a porno film show once a week, for four weeks. Fifty-one married couples watched erotic films, seventeen couples watched non-erotic films, and the rest saw no films. All couples who saw films completed eighty-four consecutive daily check lists of sexual and marital behaviour. After each erotic film show, the sexual activity of a minority of the experimental couples increased somewhat (the percentage was almost exactly the same as in the Danish experiment). Apart from that, no significant changes were found in the behaviour of those who had seen the erotic films. Even ninety minutes of porno stimulation repeated fifteen times in the course of five weeks had no other long-term effect on experimental subjects (twenty-three male students) other than a considerable lowering of both their interest in and response to pornography (Howard, Reifer and Liptzin, 1971; Howard, Liptzin and Reifer, 1973).

It is apparent that any idea of general short- or long-term detrimental effect of pornography must be rejected. At any rate, the burden of proof has been definitely shifted. Anyone who chooses to go on claiming that such harmful effects exist will have to produce evidence of his assertion. But this conclusion does not end the debate of the effects of pornography. We are still left with a very serious problem, namely the effect of pornography in unique cases. No number of experiments of the above-mentioned type can do away with the fear that in a few rare cases of 'predisposed' or 'abnormal' individuals pornography may evoke violent reactions involving serious harm to that individual, and/or to others. Even if such a thing happened only in rare cases there would still be a basis for serious concern about pornography and, perhaps, even a justification for prohibition.

The U.S. Supreme Court recently decided that a causal connection between pornography and anti-social conduct can neither be proved nor disproved. Half of this statement may be true, the other half is definitely wrong. It is true that it is almost impossible to prove that pornography directly causes sexual offences. It is well known that crime is the outcome of a complex of social and psychological factors. It is quite impossible to single out one cause. This is substantiated by an examination both of individual crimes and of the general trend in criminal statistics. If, therefore, in the Danish experience, the number of reported sexual offences had increased along with the increased availability of pornography, it would have been hard, perhaps impossible to prove that pornography was the cause of this increase. On the other hand, in the event that a high or increased availability of pornography is not accompanied by a high or increased incidence of sexual offences it is a lot easier to disprove that pornography is the cause of sexual offences. These are exactly the circumstances presented by the Danish experience: not only was there no increase in sexual offences along with the increased availability of pornography, there was in fact a very considerable decrease as the pornographic scene increased. This decrease took place in all types of sexual offences except rape, which remained unchanged (Kutchinsky, 1973b, in press).

To maintain the position that there still remains doubt as to whether or not pornography leads to sexual offences, one would have to show not only that the decrease reported in sexual offences is fictitious, but also that the statistics obscure an actual increase in the number of offences committed. Not only have attempts to cast doubt on the statistics and my interpretation of them failed, it has also become increasingly more firmly substantiated that at least in certain types of serious sexual offences, such as child molesting, the decrease in reported cases was a reflection of an actual decrease in the number of cases committed.

Moreover the Danish experience has disproved the hypothesis that pornography is dangerous even when consumed by certain 'predisposed' and 'abnormal' individuals. As far as this can be measured in terms of sexual offences, pornography is not dangerous. Quite a different question occasioned by the Danish experience is whether pornography, far from being dangerous, is beneficial; that is, was easy availability of pornography one of the factors which brought about the decrease in sex offences in Denmark? This question, too, can only be answered at greater length.

Epilogue

Pornography has come to stay in the Western World. Starting in the north, the wave has swept to other countries which are now experiencing the same uproar of publicity, curiosity and economic exploitation. In Denmark the porno wave is over. In this country pornography is mainly an export article and the producers are growing worried about the growing competition from abroad. Apart from this, pornography has found its very modest place: as something quite indifferent to most people, as entertainment and a spice in the daily life of a minority – and perhaps as important as their daily bread to a small handful of individuals.

I have no doubt that a similar development will be seen in any other country which takes the wise step of repealing the ban on pornography.

References

Alschuler, Martha: 'Origins of the law of obscenity'. *Technical report of the Commission on Obscenity and Pornography.* Vol. 2. Washington, D.C.: Government Printing Office (1971), pp. 65–81.

Goldstein, Michael J. and Wilson, W. Cody: 'Introduction'. In W. Cody Wilson and Michael J. Goldstein (Eds.): 'Pornography: Attitudes, use and effects'. *Journal of Social Issues,* (1973) **29**, (3), pp. 1–5.

Howard, James L., Reifler, Clifford B. and Liptzin, Myron B.: 'Effects of exposure to pornography'. *Technical report of the Commission on Obscenity and Por-*

nography. Vol. 8. Washington, D.C.: Government Printing Office (1971), pp. 97–132.

Howard, James L., Liptzin, Myron B. and Reifler, Clifford B.: 'Is pornography a problem?' In W. Cody Wilson and Michael J. Goldstein (Eds.): 'Pornography: Attitudes, use and effects'. *Journal of Social Issues,* (1973) **29**, (3), pp. 133–45.

Hyde, H. Montgomery: *A history of pornography*. London (1964).

Kinsey, Alfred C., Pomeroy, Wardell B., Martin, Clyde E. and Gebhard, Paul H.: *Sexual behaviour in the human female*. Philadelphia and London: Saunders 1953.

Kutchinsky, Berl: 'Eroticism without censorship. Sociological investigations on the production and consumption of pornographic literature in Denmark'. *International Journal of Criminology and Penology,* 1973, **1**, pp. 217–25, (a).

Kutchinsky, Berl: 'The effect of easy availability of pornography on the incidence of sex crimes: The Danish experience'. In W. Cody Wilson and Michael J. Goldstein (Eds.): 'Pornography: Attitudes, use and effects'. *Journal of Social Issues,* (1973) **29**, (3), pp. 163–81, (b).

Kutchinsky, Berl: *Law, pornography and crime: The Danish experience,* London: Martin Robertson, in press.

Mann, Jay, Sidman, Jack and Starr, Sheldon: 'Effects of erotic films on the sexual behavior of married couples'. *Technical report of The Commission on Obscenity and Pornography*. Vol. 8. Washington, D.C.: Government Printing Office (1971), pp. 170–254.

Mann, Jay, Sidman, Jack and Starr, Sheldon: 'Evaluating social consequences of erotic films: An experimental approach'. In W. Cody Wilson and Michael J. Goldstein (Eds.): 'Pornography: Attitudes, use and effects'. *Journal of Social Issues,* 1973, **29**, (3), pp. 113–31.

Straffelovrådets betænkning om straf for pornografi. (Report of the Danish Penal Law Committee on the punishment of pornography.) Betænkning nr. 435. København: Statens trykningskontor (1966).

The Longford Report: Pornography. London: Hodder (1972).

The report of The Commission on Obscenity and Pornography. Washington, D.C.: Government Printing Office (1970).

Waaben, Knud: 'Introduction: legislation on pornography in Denmark, Sweden and Norway'. In Berl Kutchinsky: *Law, pornography and crime: The Danish experience*. London: Martin Robertson, in press.

Therapeutic Uses of Obscenity

by Patricia Gillan

The therapeutic use of sexually stimulating or obscene material began as part of the treatment for reconditioning sexual deviants. Research therapists usually used readily available illustrations drawn from commercial sources like pornographic magazines. In the course of redirecting their sexual energies male patients were made to associate either displeasure with their deviant interest or pleasure with erotic heterosexual situations. In the early days of sex therapy, reconditioning and redirection of sexual activity was accomplished by means of aversion therapy, often in the form of electric shocks. This has gradually become much less common. The emphasis nowadays is on reward for the more approved or more desired sexual activities, rather than punishment. But the sexually deviant have proved a somewhat unrewarding group to treat and there have been gradual changes in therapeutic enthusiasm. For instance, homosexuals are no longer regarded as deviant and few wish to change.

The patients' problems which have now become the targets of therapy are the failures and dysfunctions of ordinary socially approved heterosexual behaviour. A man or woman seeks therapy because of a specific dysfunction which is handicapping him or her in a sexual relationship. In developing methods for treating previously intractable dysfunctions such as Vaginismus and Impotence, Masters and Johnson revealed a great area of need. The reduction of anxiety is considered by them to be of paramount importance. Essentially their treatment was a graduated retraining of touch, leading to genital stimulation and sexual intercourse in the F.S.P. (Female Superior Position). These methods have proved quick, effective and readily learned by experienced therapists.

However, in spite of the Masters and Johnson programme, applied

127

both in the U.S.A. and in a modified form in the U.K., there has remained a substantial number of patients who did not make as much improvement as was hoped. Amongst these cases there were many who said that they lacked any real sexual desire: a typical complaint was that 'I just do not seem to have any interest any longer'. For these cases psychologists invented the idea of 'low sex drive'. This in itself, of course, was no advance, but it led to the development of new ideas of treatment.

There were now two basic conditions clearly defined, either of which could interfere with sexual performance. The first, anxiety, was effectively treated by the Masters and Johnson regime; but the second, low sex drive, was not necessarily associated with anxiety at all and might not be any cause for complaint were it not for the fact that it imperilled marriages. Again, though low sex drive is not a generally recognised dysfunction, it is frequently considered to underlie other conditions, such as difficulties in obtaining orgasms in the female and erectile impotence in the male. In order to treat this kind of failure some means of reawakening sexual interest and appetite was essential. Sexually explicit photographs, films, books and tapes were an obvious choice, and they have proved so effective that they are now a vital adjunct to other therapeutic methods.

In this discussion I shall not discuss at any length whether sexually stimulating presentations are pornographic, obscene or merely erotic. In the literary field the distinction between that which is acceptable and that which is not acceptable is often made on the basis of whether the book concerned has literary merit or not. In other words one can accept a dose of obscenity if it is given with a dose of art. Some presentations classify themselves as obscene because of the nature of their intended aim though the same material might appear quite harmless if it occurred in a cinema adaptation of some classic. Thus the use of 'border-line taboo' material to encourage the consumption of tobacco has, in my view, been rightly regarded as immoral. I believe that the context is of crucial importance in this question, and that in the context in which I use such material I do not feel that there is any element of immorality. For this reason, I intend to use the description erotic, rather than obscene.

Erotica has been used in two types of psychological therapy:

1. *Treatment of Sexual Deviations*
   (i) Aversion Therapy – for patients who are involved in

sexually deviant practices which might result in breaking the law such as paedophilia.
(ii) Assessment of Deviations.
(iii) Reconditioning Therapy – for patients with sexual deviations.

2. *Treatment of Sexual Dysfunction*
For patients who are sexually inadequate or impotent.

Both methods of treatment use erotica to produce a positive change. The paedophiliac can be conditioned to redirect his arousal to adult partners and the impotent male patient or the 'orgasmically dysfunctional' (previously called frigid) female patient achieve greater enjoyment of sexual intercourse.

I. The Contribution of Erotica to the Treatment of Sexual Deviations

(i) *Aversion*

The principle of treating sexual deviations is to pair the deviant stimuli with a noxious event, such as an electric shock. In the case of a paedophiliac shocks are given whilst the patient is viewing slides of children or reading stories about children. Another method of aversion is to allow the patient to avoid the shock by pressing a button in order to turn on a picture of a woman or maybe a man and woman making love. This method is based on escape and avoidance training and allows the patient to avoid the shock by producing a response that stops his exposure to the deviant behaviour. The procedure can be used with 'positive conditioning' in various disorders which also include: Fetishism, Ephebophilia, Exhibitionism, Rape, Bestiality, etc. The method and the pictures used can be modified for each individual case, but the common purpose is to change the behaviour and unacceptable responses which are causing the patient to suffer, and also to redirect his behaviour along other channels. In the case of homosexuality the aim may well be to add to their repertoire the possibility of heterosexual behaviour and need not necessarily be to eliminate the homosexual element unless the patient is very insistent on this attempt.

Bancroft (1969) used photographs of males and asked his patients to imagine homosexual fantasies whilst looking at them. This was accompanied by electric shocks. Pictures of females were presented without shocks and the patient was encouraged to produce heterosexual fantasies. Ten patients showed a reduction, though not a complete absence of homosexual interest and behaviour following the treatment, and there was some increase in heterosexual interest.

It is not necessary to use visual stimuli if other stimuli are successful. Abel *et al.* (1970) successfully modified deviant behaviour by using auditory erotic stimuli. The patient could avoid the shocks by reporting aloud a fantasy of some desired sexual activity and detailed descriptions of the undesired sexual behaviour and its usual setting could be taped. These sequences allow the therapist to deliver the shock at any point he thinks important, for example, during the initiation or 'setting up' of the undesired sexual activity, when the patient might be describing himself lying in wait outside a school or near some children's swings.

(ii) *Assessment*

Erotica may be used as an assessment device. The manner in which a patient responds to an erotic stimulus may tell one more in a minute than half an hour of questioning would. Photographs of male and female nudes can be used for this purpose. Freund (1967) was the first to measure penis volume changes in response to coloured slides of nude males and females of various ages. By this method be studied the structure of erotic preference in paedophilia. He also used slides to determine the sexual orientation of male subjects and similar work was done by McConaghy (1967) who used female and male film sequences to discriminate between the heterosexual and the homosexual male.

Barr (1973) similarly used female and male erotic film sequences to study the responses of twenty-four transsexual patients and forty-four patients requesting treatment for homosexual impulses. The transsexual patients had requested 'sex change' surgery. Before such a crucial and irreversible step as sex surgery is taken, all available tests must be carried out to ensure that the patient will not regret the sex change.

Transsexuals tended to show larger galvanic skin responses to females than to males. In contrast to this they showed greater penile volume responses to males. Thus by one measure (the sweat test), the transsexuals preferred women, by a second test (the penile volume test), they preferred males. I suggest a way to understand this apparent contradiction is to believe that transsexuals have a greater overall and external interest in women and a greater sexual interest in men. A similar contradiction is seen in some 'normal' men who prefer to watch male athletics, whilst preferring female fashion.

(iii) *Reorientation or Reconditioning*

The aim of reorientation or reconditioning therapy is to establish the desired sexual behaviour in patients who for one reason or another may wish to change their orientation. Some therapists believe that sexual fantasies may be studied and used for such treatment. Rather than just presenting slides of deviant activity in association with shocks, Feldman and MacCullough (1965) stressed the importance of encouraging the patient to fantasise whilst viewing such material. It was during these fantasies that the aversion was applied. Other therapists, including Marshall (1973), went on to suggest that if fantasy plays an important part in maintaining deviant behaviour, then direct methods of modifying the fantasies should provide an effective alternative treatment to aversion for sexual deviance.

In 1968 a therapist (Davison) employed a reconditioning method for sexual deviation treatment. He asked a patient who had 'sadistic problems' to obtain an erection by the use of his sadistic fantasies and then to masturbate while looking at a picture of a sexy, nude woman in *Playboy* magazine. As orgasm was approaching, he was at all costs to focus on the *Playboy* picture, even if sadistic fantasies began to intrude.

Masturbatory fantasies can be shaped by the use of heterosexual visual or auditory erotica. For instance, Marshall used slides to help patients develop fantasies which were taped and used later; during treatment itself their penile responses to the fantasies were recorded by the penile plethysmograph. These patients were asked to use deviant fantasies to initiate masturbation, and to continue to imagine them until immediately before ejaculation, at which time they were asked to switch to the desired fantasy. The patients were asked to carry on this practice until they were able to control their fantasy content at ejaculation. The therapist then advised the patient to begin to extend the desired fantasy (previously rehearsed) back in the sequence until it would serve as the initiating stimulus. Eleven out of twelve patients were successfully treated; their undesired behaviour included: homosexuality (3 patients), fetishism (2 patients), rape (2 patients) and paedophilia (5 patients). Results indicated that for all the patients there was a reduction in the rated attractiveness of deviant fantasies, and a corresponding increase in the rated attractiveness of the appropriate fantasies at the end of the treatment. These rating changes were matched by changes in penile responses to the material.

A recent study (Herman *et al.*, 1974) shows the importance of the type of heterosexual stimuli used in the re-orientation of homosexuals. He based his re-orientation method on Marquis's (1970) technique. Marquis showed that sexual object choice can be changed through controlling masturbatory fantasies. During the process of evaluating one technique of pairing heterosexual stimuli with masturbatory activity an unexpected finding ensued. Heterosexual arousal in a homosexual patient increased sharply in a condition where he viewed a film explicitly depicting a nude, young, attractive female assuming various sexual poses. Herman used this type of erotic film in therapy. During therapy, patients were asked to imagine engaging in heterosexual behaviour with the female in the film. He also used slides of attractive males and seductive females as a baseline measure for therapy. An increase in penile response was paralleled in many instances by changes in masturbatory fantasy and reports of arousal and heterosexual behaviour outside the laboratory. Herman concluded that films seemed to be a far more powerful stimulus than slides. Patients during treatment also saw a homosexual-type film – of a Boy Scout jamboree – this was used to test their homosexual tendencies by confronting them in a controlled laboratory atmosphere. The subjects were told that if they could learn to control their homosexual arousal their heterosexual arousal would continue to increase. The next therapy step was to show them a female film again.

The above study shows the importance of the use of erotica in re-orientation therapy. Barlow (1973) has reviewed techniques for shaping and increasing heterosexual responsiveness. He questioned the application of aversion therapy in the treatment of sexual deviance and suggested that positive re-orientation techniques may be sufficient. I tend to agree.

It cannot be maintained that all the problems associated with aversion therapy have been sorted out, but, as Bancroft (1970) pointed out, when aversion therapy does work on sexual disorders it succeeds not because it decreases deviant arousal, but, paradoxically, because heterosexual responsiveness increases.

Homosexuals who wish to enter the heterosexual field of encounters can be helped to do so by the re-orientation method. It is by no means essential for this method that the homosexual should be entirely switched off his homosexual tendencies. The emphasis is solely on re-orientation. You might say that his options have been maximised.

Other re-orientation methods, such as the use of erotic tape-recorded passages, can contribute to therapy. Rosen (1974) used erotic tapes to elicit penile tumescence. In his experiment he asked male volunteers to try and diminish the strength of their erections. He showed that erections could be diminished by a contingent feedback method. I should explain what this means. The male volunteers wore a small collar around the penis which was sensitive to the degree of tumescence. The feedback was supplied by a light. When the erection reached a certain standard the light came on, when it diminished below this standard the light went off. Rosen found that if you instruct volunteers not to become erect they can inhibit their erections using this device of feedback and he used this feedback method to treat a transvestite exhibitionist. He videotaped a thirty-minute sequence in which the patient masturbated to orgasm in his customary female outfit. He then instructed this patient to diminish his erections when re-viewing this videotape by using the feedback of an alarm. Results showed that two months after the first phase of treatment he has had satisfactory sexual relations with his wife and is not turning to transvestite exhibitionism.

II. The Use of Erotica in the Therapy for Sexual Dysfunction

Most of the literature concerning the treatment of sexual dysfunction stresses the importance of anxiety and tends to neglect sexual drive or libido. In 1971 Bancroft published a paper suggesting that failure of sexual performance could be caused by low sexual drive and/or anxiety. This paper attempts to examine the problem of increasing the sexual drive of patients by the use of erotica.

Other research workers, mainly German and American have shown that exposure to sexual material results in increased sexual activity – as measured by frequency of masturbation (Amoroso) and also heterosexual coitus (Kutchinsky, Schmidt and Sigusch). Mann *et al.* found that couples who saw erotic films reported that they had benefited by an improvement in their marital and sexual relationships. These studies have been carried out on a non-patient population, usually consisting of students.

However, few studies have investigated the effect of erotica on sexually dysfunctional patients. Lehman claimed that visual material of masturbation could help orgasmically dysfunctional women. Lobitz and LoPiccolo reported that thirteen out of thirteen female patients with primary orgasmic dysfunction (that is they had never experienced an orgasm) and three out of nine women patients with secondary orgasmic dysfunction (that is they had stopped getting orgasms) were successfully treated by a programme which included supplementing a masturbation course with heterosexual erotic pictures or literature. They also mentioned that three different women in the masturbation programme reported masturbating to their first orgasm shortly after having viewed an X-film that they happened to see at the local cinema. They also successfully treated four out of six male patients with erectile failure and six out of six patients with premature ejaculation by including the use of erotic stimuli from literature, pictures and/or fantasy in their programme. Their stimulus materials ranged from heterosexual erotic materials to homosexual fantasies. The method used is for the patient to masturbate or have sexual intercourse with a partner and enjoy his fantasies. Just prior to orgasm he is asked to switch his focus to the imagined or real sexual activity with his partner. Later he is instructed to make the switch at progressively earlier points in the sexual sequence either fantasied or actual. This could be described as a progressive reintegration of the actual partner into the sexual act from which she had been excluded in fantasy. In the jargon of the psychologists the sexually dysfunctional male's partner has become the C.S. (conditioned stimulus).

My own work with patients was the first in Europe and was reported at the E.A.B.P. meeting (Gillan, 1973). My general approach was to stimulate the appetites of sexually inadequate patients by any method that was socially acceptable. Pictures of 'heterosexual activity', such as are commonly circulated in London, were shown. Stories taken from such books as *Memoirs of the Life of Fanny Hill* by John Cleland or *Lady Chatterley's Lover* by D. H. Lawrence and current literature and magazines were read by the patients. A Japanese tape recording called 'Japanese Sounds of Sex' in which women experience the ecstasy of orgasms, was played to the patients. In addition erotic films were recommended, e.g. *Belle de Jour, Danish Blue, Quiet Days in Clichy*. Lastly some stimulating music was recommended for patients to listen and maybe make love to, such as some Indian evening ragas, reggae, Ravel's *Bolero*. Patients were also asked to talk about and improve their masturbatory fantasies and techniques. Oral sex was discussed and patients were encouraged to practice this at home. Patients were also individually treated by a battery of methods which included the above techniques to increase sexual drive. Systematic desensitisation, which consists of visualising images of sexual situations drawn from a hierarchy of items (maybe ranging from holding hands to having sexual intercourse) and thinking about previous difficulties whilst relaxing, was included, as well as a modified 'Masters and Johnson treatment'. Patients were seen conjointly once a week.

Results showed that after an average of fifteen sessions eight impotent men out of ten improved. The criterion of improvement was whether a patient could obtain an erection, enter the vagina and ejaculate by the end of treatment. Patients with premature ejaculations were not included in this study. There were six cases of secondary and four cases of primary impotence and the two failures came one from each group.

In my second study (Gillan, 1974) an attempt was made to control some of the variables of the previous study. Erotic stimuli together with relaxation were used as treatment for this trial and no other treatment was given. Two groups treated by erotic stimuli and a control group were drawn up as follows:

Group 1 **Visual Stimuli:** this group was presented with erotic pictures and slides of couples making love, and of male and female nudes. Photographs of paintings were included, Allen Jones's work, ancient Japanese erotic prints, and the like.

Group 2 **Auditory Stimuli:** patients were asked to silently read erotic literature (old and new). Stories from *Vibrations* and *New Dimensions* were included, as well as articles and letters from *Forum*. Patients were also asked to listen to Japanese sex tapes and to develop and write their own erotic fantasies.

Group 3 **Control Group:** patients were asked to talk about their sex problems, but an effort was made to steer them away from this and to discuss other non-sexual topics.

All the patients in the above groups received deep relaxation and this was always given for fifteen minutes at the beginning of each session. Each patient attended alone, without a partner, and sex treatment sessions were given after one case-history-taking session.

As impotent male patients had responded so well to treatment in my previous study (Gillan, 1973) I felt that sexually inadequate female patients should be included in the second study. The women included could be divided into two groups: the first group had no feelings of pleasure when sexual intercourse took place and some even disliked being touched, and did not enjoy foreplay or want insertion. Other women patients found sexual intercourse pleasant but could not reach a climax as they were suffering from orgasmic dysfunction. The men could also be classified into two groups: those who had erectile failure and could not get an erection, and those who lost their erection when insertion took place.

Finally there were fourteen males and ten females allocated as randomly as possible in the three groups, making a total of twenty-four patients. (A balanced sex distribution would have been preferable, in that men are supposed to repond more than women to erotic audio-visual stimuli.)

Table 1. *Classification of the sexual dysfunction of the 24 patients*

DISORDER	VISUAL	AUDITORY	CONTROL	TOTAL
No erection	3	3	4	10
Impotent inside	2	1	1	4
Orgasmic dysfunction	1	2	2	5
No pleasure	2	2	1	5
TOTAL	8	8	8	24

Assessment before and after treatment was carefully considered. Measures were also taken one month after treatment had ended. Measures included ratings on the international sex scales, devised by Chabot, to assess feelings during sexual intercourse, sexual intercourse frequency, and also sexual relationship with partner. Patients' initial reactions to erotic audio-visual material were also assessed before treatment by rating a picture of heterosexual intercourse on a 'pleasure scale', likewise an erotic story (e.g. excerpts from *Fanny Hill*) was assessed. All the patients were given similar stories and pictures after treatment and at follow-up, parallel material was presented so as to control for habituation. The sexual intercourse pictures were chosen as they were considered stimulating and acceptable by the author and her husband. This actually supported Byrne's findings that husbands and wives respond in a similar manner to erotica and tend to like and enjoy the same type of stimulus.

The results were as follows:

1. The patients in Groups 1 and 2 (Visual and Auditory) improved. These were the groups which received stimulation (see Figs. 1, 2 and 3).
2. Groups 1 and 2 did not differ; in other words visual stimuli patients were not superior to auditory stimuli patients or vice versa (see Figs. 1, 2 and 3).
3. Group 3 (Control), the group which did not receive stimulation treatment, did not improve (see Figs. 1, 2 and 3).
4. Groups 1 and 2 showed improvement rated by:
   (i) frequency of sexual intercourse (Fig. 1).
   (ii) a rating of sexual feelings (Fig. 2).
   (iii) state of the sexual relationship with partner (Fig. 3).
5. There was no difference between the sexes in response to the two different modes of stimulation (i.e. visual and auditory).

DISCUSSION

(i) *Measures*

In this study patients and therapists made ratings of performance and sexual feeling. Ratings made by an external assessor should also have been included, but this was not possible. Ideally, psycho-physiological measures should have been taken, but at the time of the study a good psycho-physiological measure of sexual response was not available for women. For men the penile plethysmograph has proved satisfactory.

It would be possible to envisage the use of an *in vivo* measure of sexual performance – such as has been used by Masters and Johnson (1966). However the difficulties, both social and personal, make this

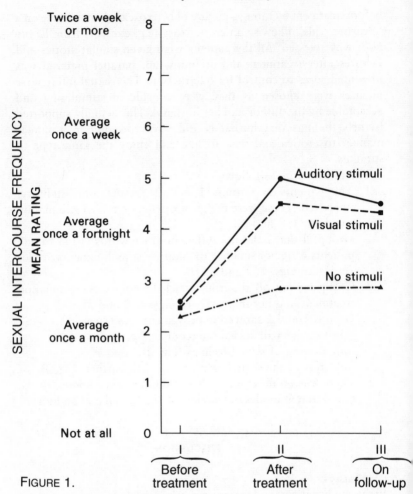

FIGURE 1.

an almost impossible measure to use. Lazarus (1963) had similar objections to the use of such an 'avoidance test'. Gillan and Rachman (1974) have discussed the difficulties of assessment and the importance of a behavioural evidence test in which the patient is asked to approach or enter into the fearful situation.

Although frequency of sexual intercourse was used as a measure of success, it is not entirely satisfactory. Whilst even a slight degree of impotence is a serious barrier to sexual intercourse, quite a considerable degree of fear and dysfunction in the female does not

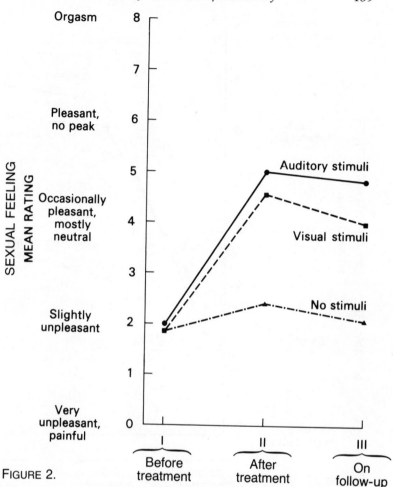

FIGURE 2.

prevent sexual intercourse either before or after treatment. The author is satisfied that frequency of sexual intercourse is a good change measure for use with men. Whereas the achievement of orgasm is a good measure for women it fails for men, as some patients ejaculate whilst flaccid and find it unsatisfactory.

(ii) *Male/Female Response Similarity*
Kinsey (1953) found that males had a greater predisposition to arousal to external stimuli than females. In the present study, on the

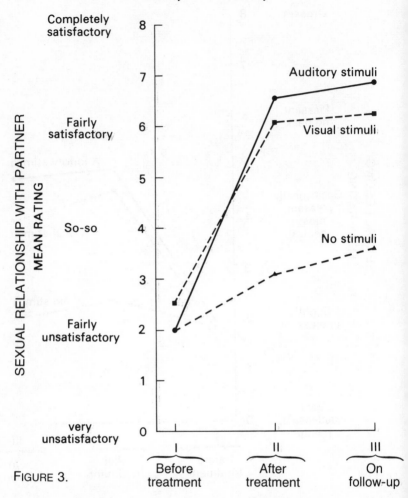

FIGURE 3.

contrary, no difference is shown. Concerning auditory erotic stimuli, several pieces of work have tended to show that women respond equally or more than men to auditory stimuli. Jakobovits (1965) made a similar finding in that the women in his study were significantly more stimulated by pornographic literature than men. Schmidt, Sigusch and Schafer (1972) found only slight differences between males and females in response to erotic stories, but found that in the ensuing 24 hours females showed greater sexual activity than the males.

The findings for visual stimuli are also of interest – again Kinsey's work suggests that males are more readily aroused by a wide range of visual stimuli. The present research work shows that males and females do not differ. The slight difference in favour of males was not significant. It could be ascribed to the nature of the material used as stimuli. It has been found, for instance, by Byrne and Lambeth (1970) that females were more aroused when asked to imagine activities on themes of masculine stimuli: male nudity, male masturbation, fellatio between males. Sigusch *et al.* (1970) showed that males are more aroused than females in response to pictures showing solitary figures. Mosher (1970) reported that men were significantly more aroused than women by pictures of oral sex. The stimuli used in this study were pictures of normal heterosexual activity, oral sex and pin-ups of both sexes. No pictures of male masturbation or fellatio between males were included. It is thus possible that the material could have been biased in favour of male responsiveness.

For assessment rating pictures of coitus were used. No sex differences for this type of material have been reported (Mosher). It is thus reasonable to think that the assessment pictures were unbiased.

As the presentation material of sexual interest in the present study was chosen by the author and her husband, perhaps this could help to explain the similarity of response. It may be that in other studies women were not consulted over the choice of stimuli. For more definitive work it would be necessary to select the material with reference to more opinions. In any further study both the material included and that excluded must be carefully specified. In this study pictures involving children, animals and cruelty were excluded.

The type of material used in studies of erotica should be carefully chosen. According to some studies (Corman, 1968; Davis & Buchwald, 1957; Levitt, 1969; Schmidt & Sigusch, 1972; Schmidt *et al.*, 1972) films are more arousing than photographs, which in turn are more stimulating than books and stories. Levitt found nudes more arousing than clothed figures and photographs more arousing than drawings.

In view of the above it is surprising that the auditory material was so effective. It should be said, however, that the material labelled 'auditory' in the study was not exclusively so. The stories were read silently, and one cannot be sure that as stimuli they would be equivalent to the same material read aloud. The same criticism applies to the 'development of sexual fantasies' as these fantasies were written, rather than spoken. Fantasies can be regarded as a powerful stimulus on their own in that Byrne and Lambeth (1970) have stressed that imaginary situations can be more effective than photographs or literary descriptions in providing sexual arousal. Bancroft and Mathews (1971) support this finding that fantasy is important for sexual arousal. It could be argued that the 'Sounds of Sex' tape, although exclusively auditory, is more stimulating than any other auditory material used for arousal. This again may explain the success of the present 'auditory' material.

(iii) *The Use of Erotic Stimuli in Treatment*

'Stimulation therapy' appears to help, but not sufficiently in the findings of the present study to cure patients; possibly the treatment period was too short. Just under half the patients went on afterwards to treatment composed of modified Masters and Johnson techniques, systematic desensitisation, oral sex instructions, and audio-visual stimuli. Most of the controls were treated by this method. This resulted in a high success rate with three out of four of the last group of patients showing improvement.

Another recent study in the U.K. by Asirdas and Beech (1974) used erotic slides, fantasies, a tape recording and the vibrator as erotic stimuli. All these erotica contributed to the successful treatment of patients, twelve men with problems of impotence and twelve women suffering from orgasmic dysfunction. The erotic stimuli group was called the 'positive conditioning' group – as this represented an attempt to transfer sexual arousal from an existing adequate stimulus to the complex stimulus of sexual intercourse with a partner where, currently, the patient was unable to react effectively. The erotica were used to produce sexual arousal so as to effect the transfer of such feelings to the partner. The results indicated substantial improvement in physical responsivity, attitudes concerning sexuality and behavioural measures, for both treatments, with positive conditioning showing more promise than systematic desensitisation. This again shows the importance of erotica in treatment. There were no sex differences in response to treatment.

Recently French therapists too have enthused over the use of erotica in treatment. Zwang and Romieu (1974) recommend pictures of sex in groups, but exclude the worse deviations of homosexuality and sado-masochism. They suggested the use of erotic books and stated that 'the stimulating effect of erotica operates for both sexes, contrary to received opinion: in women erotica is capable of aiding the production of vaginal lubrication – which looking at a knitting magazine cannot do'. They also claim that films designed to excite people can be therapeutic in their own way, and home projection should be encouraged, as well as communal baths, a mirror by the side of the bed, gastronomic outings, and learning about pleasure and hedonism. They lastly state that sexual pleasure is 'the pleasure of the senses and nothing is worse than sensual frustration'.

More evidence in favour of erotic films for therapy is coming from the U.S.A. Couples are helped to overcome their sexual problems by viewing such films. Renick (1973) described the use of films showing sexual intercourse shown during therapy. The treatment he describes is based on Hartman and Fithian's method of showing patients films of couples in different coital positions or non-demand sexual techniques. This method, as well as Renick's method, of showing his patients the films before they are asked to engage in that particular activity, so as to provide a possible 'model' for them, has had favourable results. Sayner and Durrell (1975) reduce anxiety related to sexual activity by asking couples to sit together through hours of pornographic films, or to read sexually explicit books together. The above therapists report success with this desensitisation method, but neither study includes a 'control' group.

The best American controlled study has been done in Hawaii by Robinson (1974). The women treated had problems of anorgasmia, either primary or secondary. Robinson compared film treatment on videotapes, with a control group drawn from his waiting list. Fourteen out of fifteen women increased their frequency of masturbation after viewing videotapes of a therapist and a couple discussing self-stimulation, or masturbation techniques associated with orgasm. Five out of six women who had never masturbated before started doing so after viewing the tapes. Two variations of the videotape treatment programme included three tapes on 'attitudes and general information about sex'; three tapes of specific suggestions about self-stimulation or masturbation. Further treatment involving verbal suggestions resulted in fourteen out of fifteen women reporting either the occurrence of their first orgasm or an increase in the frequency of orgasm.

On the basis of these studies we can conclude that (1) erotica contributes to the treatment of sexual deviations by aversion therapy or by re-orientation therapy; (2) erotica can also be helpful in the diagnosis or assessment of disorders; (3) the use of erotica is also important in 'stimulation therapy', as there is evidence that it enhances sexual pleasure and performance and helps patients to function again.

Erotica is clearly very useful to the therapist, but hostile attitudes to such material on the part of many influential members of society remain a problem.

The Attitude of Society to the Use of Erotic Stimuli

This paper will probably be under fire when the Establishment realises that erotic stimuli have been used to help patients function again. It is our society that is at fault. British culture and other cultures which have been strongly influenced by Christianity and Judaism contain large elements of sexual repressiveness, associated with authoritarianism. It is not surprising that the Christian Church, with its predominantly male and authoritarian hierarchy, has come to frown on sexual behaviour in which women necessarily have such a large part. The penalty for the exclusion of women and the free expression of sexuality is the need for harsh taboos. Of course a harsh taboo may be expressed as a law or just as a 'don't' (thus little boys caught with their hands down the front of their trousers touching their genitals are reprimanded and warned not to play pocket billiards). The authoritarian and hierarchical structure of the church has influenced most of our institutions – it is all too plain in Government, Industry, Schools and Nursing. The maintenance of the pyramid is all important. These overbearing institutions change slowly and those at the top do not wish to change at all. To flout the rules at any point, however small, is to threaten the whole structure. A pornography book or photography of sexual intercourse is such a challenge. A challenge, which, although apparently small and human, needs to be met with police raids and new laws. The authorities fear not only that society will be upset and that people will actually enjoy themselves, but also perhaps they fear the power of sex within themselves, the feelings they have been taught to repress.

One argument to be overcome is this: could the promotion of pornography lead to an increase in sexual offences, as defined even by the most liberal, for instance rape, or sexual offences against children? The relaxation of laws against pornography in Scandinavia has not led to such an increase. Kutchinsky (1970) found declines in certain classes of sex offence behaviour in Denmark following the liberalisation of their pornography laws. I think it would be the view of most of my colleagues that repressive attitudes towards sex, especially during upbringing, are just as likely to promote such crimes. In the Marquesan Islands near Tahiti, the children not only watch their parents making love but also are masturbated. In the islands' history there is no record of rape or sexual violence. Bryant, of the Institute of Sexual Education in Florida, stated that he believed that human violence in nations, as well as in human beings, springs from repressed emotions.

Whatever the authorities may wish, the liberalisation of sexual attitudes within society proceeds apace. With the lifting of repression and with the rise in standards of education the part that can be played by natural sexual development in a happy life is more appreciated. More people have begun to ask themselves 'is my sex life as good as it could be?' At last the more serious failures in sexual adjustment are being treated. The marvellous work of pioneers such as Pavlov, Wolpe, Masters and Johnson, has evolved the methods. Therapists working in this field have begun to employ erotica, which would have previously been caled pornographic or obscene, to aid them in their work, to help in the redirection and maximisation of sexual drives and to increase human happiness.

REFERENCES

Abel, G. G., Levis, D. J. and Clancy, J. 'Aversion therapy applied to taped sequences of deviant behaviour in exhibitionism and other sexual deviations: a preliminary report'. *Journal of Behavioural Therapy and Experimental Psychiatry,* (1970), **1,** pp. 59–66.
Amoroso, D. M., Brown, M., Preusse, M., Ware, E. W. and Pilkey, D. W. 'An Investigation of Behavioural, Psychological and Physiological Reactions to Pornographic Stimuli'. *Technical Reports of the Commission on Obscenity and Pornography,* vol. 8, (1970), U.S. Government Printing Office, Washington D.C., p. 1.
Asirdas, S. and Beech, H. R. 'The treatment of sexual inadequacy'. Paper presented at The Society for Psychosomatic Res. 18th Ann. Conference, (1974).
Bancroft, J. 'Aversion Therapy of Homosexuality: A Pilot Study of Ten Cases'. *British Journal of Psychiatry,* (1969), **115,** pp. 1417–31.

Bancroft, J. In *Behaviour Therapy in the 1970's*. Eds. L. E. Bunn and J. L. Wosley, (1970).

Bancroft, J. 'Sexual Inadequacy in the Male'. *Postgraduate Medical Journal*, (1971), **47**, pp. 562–71.

Bancroft, J. and Mathews, A. 'Autonomic correlates of penile erection'. *Journal of Psychosomatic Research*, (1971), **15**, pp. 159–67.

Barlow, D. H. 'Increasing aversive heterosexual responsiveness'. *Behavioural Therapy*, (1973), 4.

Barr, R. F. 'Responses to Erotic Stimuli of Transsexual and Homosexual Males'. *Brit. J. Psychiat.*, (1973), **123**, pp. 579–85.

Byrne, D., Lambeth, J. 'The effect of erotic stimuli on sex arousal, evaluative responses, and subsequent behaviour'. In *Technical Report of the Commission on Obscenity and Pornography*. Vol. 8, (1970), Washington, D.C., U.S. Government Printing Office.

Corman, C. *Physiological Response to a Sexual Stimulus*. Unpublished B.Sc. Thesis. University of Manitoba, (1968).

Davis, R. C. and Buchwald, A. M. *J. Comp. physiol. Psychol.*, (1957), pp. 50, 44.

Davison, G. C. Case Report. 'Elimination of a sadistic fantasy by a client-controlled counter-conditioning technique'. *Journal of Abnormal Psychology*, (1968), vol. 73, No. 1, pp. 84–90.

Feldman, M. P. and MacCulloch, M. C. 'The application of anticipatory avoidance learning to the treatment of homosexuality. 1. Theory, techniques and preliminary results'. *Behav. Res. Ther.*, (1965), **2**, pp. 165–83.

Freund, K. 'Erotic Preference in Pedophilia'. *Behav. Res. & Therapy*, (1967), vol. 5, pp. 339–48.

Freund, K. and Costell, R. 'The structure of erotic preference in the non-deviant male'. *Behav. Res. & Ther.*, (1970), vol. 8, pp. 15–20.

Gillan, P. 'Behavioural re-education in impotence'. Paper presented at the European Association of Behavioural Psychotherapy Conference, Amsterdam, (1973).

Gillan, P. 'Impotence, Frigidity and Erotic Stimuli'. Paper presented at European Association of Behavioural Psychotherapy Conference, (1974).

Gillan, P. and Gillan, R. *Sex Therapy Today*. Open Books, (1976).

Gillan, P. and Rachman, S. 'An experimental investigation of Desensitization in Phobic Patients'. *Brit. Jul. Psychiatry*, (1974), vol. 124.

Herman, S. H., Barlow, D. H. and Agras, W. S. 'An experimental analysis of classical conditioning as a method of increasing heterosexual arousal in homosexuals'. *Behav. Res. Ther.* (1974) vol. 12.

Jakobovits. 'Evaluational reactions to erotic literature'. *Psychol. Rep.*, (1965), **16**, pp. 985–94.

Kinsey, A. C., Pomeroy, W. B. and Martin, C. E. *Sexual behaviour in the Human Female*. Philadelphia: W. B. Saunders Co., (1953).

Kutchinsky, B. 'Sex Crimes and Pornography in Copenhagen: A Study of Attitudes'. *Technical Reports of the Commission on Obscenity and Pornography*, 7, U.S. Government Printing Office, Washington D.C. (1970), p. 263.

Lazarus, A. A. 'The results of behaviour therapy in 126 cases of severe neurosis'. *Behav. Res. Ther.* (1963), **1**, pp. 69–79.

Lazarus, A. A. and Rosen, R. C. 'Behaviour therapy techniques in the treatment of sexual disabilities'. Chapter in *Forms of direct intervention in sexual problems*. J. K. Meyer (ed.). Medcom Publ. (1974).

Lehman, R. E. 'The disinhibiting effects of visual material in treating orgasmically dysfunctional women'. *Behav. Engineering*, (1973).

Levitt, E. E. *J. Sex Research*, (1969), **5**, p. 247.

Levitt, E. E. and Brady, J. P. *Clin. Psychol.* (1965), **21**, p. 347.

Lobitz, W. C. and LoPiccolo, J. 'New methods in the behavioural treatment of sexual dysfunction'. *J. Behav. Ther. & Exp. Psychiat.* (1972), vol. 3, pp. 265–71.

Mann, J., Sidman, J. and Starr, S. 'Effects of erotic films on sexual behaviour of married couples. *Technical reports of the commission on obscenity and pornography*, vol. 8, (1970), U.S. Government Printing Office.

Marquis, J. N. 'Orgasmic re-conditioning: changing sexual object choice through controlling masturbation fantasies'. *J. Behav. Ther. & Exp. Psychiat.*, 1, pp. 263–71.

Marshall, W. L. 'The modification of sexual fantasies: a combined treatment approach to the reduction of deviant sexual behaviour'. *Behav. Res. & Therapy*, (1973), vol. 11, pp. 557–64.

Masters, W. H. and Johnson, V. E. *Human Sexual Response.* Little, Brown, Boston, (1966).

Masters, W. H. and Johnson, V. E. *Human Sexual Inadequacy.* Little, Brown, Boston, (1970).

McConaghy, N. 'Penile volume change to moving pictures of male and female nudes in heterosexual and homosexual subjects'. *Behav. Res. & Therapy*, (1967), 5, pp. 43–8.

Mosher, D. L. 'Physiological reactions to pornographic films'. *Technical reports of the commission on Obscenity & Pornography*, vol. 8, (1970), U.S. Government Printing Office, Washington, D.C., p. 255.

Renick, J. T. 'The use of films and videotapes in the treatment of sexual dysfunction'. Paper presented at the 81st Annual Convention of the American Psychological Association, Montreal, (1973).

Robinson, C. H. *The effects of observational learning on sexual behaviors and attitudes in orgasmic dysfunctional women.* (Doctoral dissertation, University of Hawaii, 1974). *Dissertation Abstracts International*, (1975), 35, (9B), (University Microfilms No. 75–5040, 221).

Rosen, R. C. 'The control of penile tumescence in the human male'. Symposium Presentation: 82nd Annual Convention of the APA. New Orleans, Louisiana, (1974).

Sayner, R. and Durrell, D. 'Multiple behavior therapy techniques in the treatment of sexual dysfunction'. *The Counseling Psychologist*, (1975), 5, 38–41.

Schmidt, G. and Sigusch, V. In: *Critical Issues in Contemporary Behaviour* (ed. Money, J. and Zubin, J.). Johns Hopkins Univ. Press, Balt., (1972).

Schmidt, G., Sigusch, V. and Schafer, S. *Arch. Sex. Behav.*, (1972), 2. In press.

Sigusch, V., Schmidt, G., Reinfeld, A. and Wiedmann-Sutor, J. 'Psychosexual stimulation: Sex differences'. *J. Sex. Res.*, (1970), 6, 10–24.

Zwang, G. and Romieu, A. *Précis de therapeutique sexologique.* Maloise, S.A. Ed., (1974).

Psychology and Obscenity: a Factual Look at Some of the Problems

by H. J. Eysenck

There is a general law in psychology which relates to attitudes, and in particular to the strength with which attitudes are held; it reads like this:

> When, in a group of persons, there are influences acting both in the direction of acceptance and of rejection of a belief, the result is not to make the majority adopt a lower degree of conviction, but to make some hold the belief with a high degree of conviction, while others reject it also with a high degree of conviction.

This 'principle of certainty', as Thouless called it, has much experimental evidence behind it; it will also appeal intuitively to all those who have ever argued about political, or religious, or social questions with people not holding their particular opinions.

This law clearly applies to discussions of pornography and obscenity; there usually is a clear-cut separation of the 'progressive, permissive, anti-censorship' group and the Longford-Whitehouse-Holbrook group, with hardly anyone in the middle. This polarisation of attitudes bears out the Thouless law, and consequently pleases psychologists, but it does not lead to meaningful discourse; the adversary principle of controversy takes over, and instead of seeking for the truth, both sides produce arguments, and cite evidence, only in an endeavour to gain points and controvert the opposition. This is a political, not a scientific way of proceeding; the scientist is trained to look at all the evidence, evaluate it carefully, and only then come to a conclusion which at best will be provisional, and hedged about with disclaimers. Such an approach is welcomed by neither party; they usually much prefer to get on with the fisticuffs, and never mind the umpire!

What, then, is 'obscene' and 'pornographic'? Can we define these terms at all in an agreed fashion? The term 'obscene', while sometimes used as equivalent to pornographic by laymen and dictionary-makers alike, has a different legal connotation. Some pornography is obscene, but not all; a slight case of the pornographics is not offensive, while even a slight case of the obscenities is – by definition. The definition of what was regarded as obscene used to be related to certain assumed behavioural effects, i.e. whether 'the tendency of the matter charged as obscenity is to deprave and corrupt those whose minds are open to corruption, and into whose hands a publication of this sort may fall'. These matters have since been changed in Britain, but what I wish to discuss is the psychological meaning of this 'tendency to deprave and corrupt'. Volumes have been written on this, but usually by lawyers, writers, politicians, journalists, sociologists, and others without much knowledge of the psychological literature. This seems odd, as this clearly is a purely psychological question; yet I cannot recollect any psychologist ever being asked his opinion! (Psychiatrists and psychoanalysts occasionally get a look in, not because they are supposed to know anything about psychology, but because they are medically qualified; why their medical knowledge should qualify them to speak on such a technical subject has never been clear to me.)

In a little experiment I conducted, several hundred intelligent and co-operative students were asked which of a number of activities they considered 'depraved and corrupt' (such activities only make sense in relation to a particular type of person – having intercourse with an innocent young girl is one thing, having it with a mature widow may be quite another – and consequently types of persons involved have been indicated in each case). [cf. Table 1].

Some people – mostly introverts – sprinkled ticks liberally. Seemingly they disapproved of all sexual activities outside the marital union. Even within that union, anything going beyond the 'missionary position' was condemned. Others – mostly extraverts – had only a few crosses, indicating that as far as they were concerned 'anything goes', provided it is within the law; rape and the seduction of a minor tended to be frowned upon even by the most 'enlightened'. Most respondents tended to come in between these two extremes, but their notions of depravity were clearly not identical either; indeed, the spectrum of opinion goes right across the board, from one extreme of permissiveness to the other extreme of puritanism,

Table 1. *Below are listed a number of activities of adult males towards different types of females. For each female type please place tick in the appropriate box IF YOU CONSIDER THAT THE ACTIVITY TOWARDS THAT PARTICULAR FEMALE TYPE IS EITHER DEPRAVED OR CURRUPT.*

N.B. *There are five female types to be rated for each activity. Do not make any mark if you do not consider the activity to be depraved or corrupt.*

ACTIVITY (of adult male) towards	FEMALE TYPE				
	A	B	C	D	E
	A 15 year old virgin	A 25 year old virgin	An un-married non virgin	(Husband) to married woman	(Man other than husband) to married woman
1. Kiss on the mouth					
2. Seduce					
3. Have intercourse normal fashion					
4. Lend pornographic books					
5. Touch and kiss sexual parts					
6. Initiate into prosti-tution and live on immoral earnings					
7. Take to strip-tease show					
8. Take to watch couple having intercourse					
9. Take to see blue films					
10. Vigorous petting					
11. Take to theatre in which male actors simulate intercourse					
12. Exhibit sexual parts to females					

13.	Make female dress up in clothes

14.	Take to an orgiastic party

15.	Use four-letter words

16.	Rape: force to have intercourse

without a break anywhere. There is no evidence here of that substratum of reasonable agreement on which the law seems to rely.

This is an important conclusion, though perhaps not an unexpected one; people differ widely in their standards of sexual conduct, and in the attitudes they take in this field. We have continued work on this topic, asking random samples of young and old, male and female, married and unmarried, large numbers of questions concerning their attitudes to a wide variety of sexual matters, as well as their own sexual experiences and behaviours; at the same time we administered personality questionnaires to these people. The sex questions were analysed statistically, and we found that various groups of them tended to hang together. Thus items relating to pornography tended all to be answered in one direction (favourable or unfavourable) by any particular respondent. Similarly, people tended to answer questions relating to impersonal sex either in an approving or a disapproving fashion. Twelve such factors were found in all, and these in turn were related to each other in a fairly commonsensical manner, as is indicated in Fig. 1. There are two major dimensions along which we can stratify sexual attitudes and behaviours; one is sexual libido, i.e. strength and direct expression of sexual desire, while the other is sexual satisfaction, i.e. the degree to which a person is content and satisfied with his or her sexual life. The libido factor is made up of such groups of items as impersonal sex, pornography, permissiveness, sexual excitement, aggressive sex, while its opposite, lack of libido, is associated with prudishness, sexual disgust, and sexual shyness. The satisfaction factor is positively associated with satisfaction, pleasure in physical sex, and sexual excitement, and negatively with neurotic sex, shyness, disgust, and prudishness. What is interesting and important to note here is that libido and satisfaction are quite unrelated; the degree of

152   *Censorship and Obscenity*

a person's satisfaction in the sexual field does not depend in the slightest on his libido! Strong sexual desires, and a drive for their direct expression through impersonal sex, pornographic reading and viewing, and promiscuity neither guarantee sexual satisfaction, nor do they condemn a person to eternal unhappiness. Pornography, in particular, seems to be as popular (or unpopular!) with persons who are satisfied with their sex lives as with those who are dissatisfied.

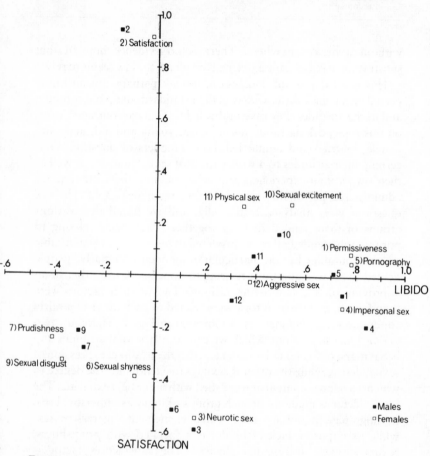

FIGURE 1

These sex attitude factors are related to personality; as I have pointed out in *Psychology is about People,* extraverts tend to be high on the libido factor, introverts weak; people who are somewhat emotional and neurotic tend to be low on satisfaction, stable people somewhat high. There is one other difference which is important: men tend to be higher on libido than women. In fact, when we pick out the items which best discriminate between men and women, they are precisely the items which measure out libido factor! A sample of such items is given in Table 2, with the high libido answers in italics. Figure 2 gives the distribution of scores for men and women respectively. Two things will be quite clear to anyone looking at this figure. Men and women differ profoundly, although there is of course some overlap. And within each sex there are tremendous differences in attitudes to sexual matters. These differences are, in part at least, due to genetic causes; we have repeated these studies with identical and fraternal twins, and found marked genetic effects, probably mediated through personality which is known to be influenced by heredity to a very marked degree. This point is fundamental to any appreciation of the problems raised by obscenity and pornography; we cannot assume that fundamentally all people are alike in their reactions to such material, and their estimation of them, provided we could only give them all the same education or social environment. People are innately different in their reactions and behaviours, and exposing them to a uniform environment would not equalise these individual differences. The puritan and the libertine, it is true, are not born puritan or libertine, but they do inherit a strong predisposition to so interact with their environment that they will grow up to embrace views at opposite ends of our libido continuum. No single set of rules or laws can appeal equally to both sides, and some compromise is therefore necessary unless we are willing (as certain societies have in the past been willing) to effectively disenfranchise one side or the other.

Our first point, then, is that people in our culture differ in their attitudes, in their behaviour, and in what they regard as 'obscene'; we must next enquire into whether the reading of certain types of literature, or the viewing of certain types of films, can influence a person's attitudes or behaviour. Much experimental work has been done in regard to this question (mostly by the American President's Commission on the Effects of Obscenity and Pornography), and much argument has raged around it, mostly poorly informed. Is it

Table 2

	Agree	*Disagree*
Sex without love ('impersonal sex') is highly unsatisfactory	Agree	*Disagree*
Conditions have to be just right to get me excited sexually	Yes	*No*
Sometimes it has been a problem to control my sex feelings	*Yes*	No
I do not need to respect a woman (man), or love her (him), in order to enjoy petting and/or intercourse with her (him)	*Yes*	No
It doesn't take much to get me excited sexually	*True*	False
I think about sex almost every day	*Yes*	No
The thought of a sex orgy is disgusting to me	Yes	*No*
I like to look at sexy pictures	*Yes*	No
Seeing a person nude doesn't interest me	True	*False*
I believe in taking my pleasures where I find them	*Yes*	No
If I had the chance to see people making love without being seen, I would take it	*Yes*	No
Pornographic writings should be freely allowed to be published	*Yes*	No
Prostitution should be legally permitted	*Yes*	No
There should be no censorship, on sexual grounds, of plays and films	*Agree*	Disagree
Absolute faithfulness to one partner throughout life is nearly as silly as celibacy	*Yes*	No
I would enjoy watching my usual sex partner having intercourse with someone else	*Yes*	No
Sex is more exciting with a stranger	*Yes*	No
To me, few things are more important than sex	*Yes*	No
Group sex appeals to me	*Yes*	No
The thought of an illicit relationship excites me	*Yes*	No
The idea of 'wife swapping' is extremely distasteful to me	Yes	*No*
I can take sex and I can leave it alone	Yes	*No*
Some forms of love-making are disgusting to me	Yes	*No*
If you are invited to see a 'blue' film, you would	*Accept*	Refuse
If you were offered a highly pornographic book, you would	*Accept*	Refuse
If you were invited to take part in an orgy, you would	*Accept*	Refuse

true that unlimited freedom for writers, painters, film-makers and all others to produce and publish without let or hindrance pornographic wares of one kind or another leads to an increase in the number of sex crimes? Denmark's statistics (a decrease in sex crimes amounting to some 22%) need to be examined critically but at least it seems to indicate that those who feared a great upsurge of sexual viciousness

Number of Subjects:

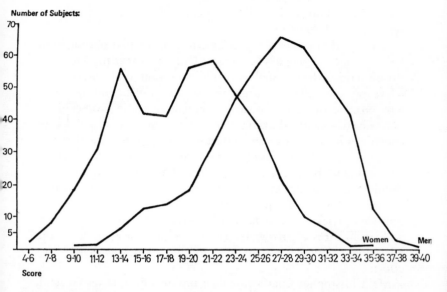

FIGURE 2 *Scores of men and women on masculinity-femininity sex attitudes inventory*

and lawlessness as a consequence of great permissiveness have been disappointed. Whether such permissiveness actually produces a reduction in crimes cannot be finally asserted yet.

Can we claim then that greater permissiveness in the publication of pornography has no effect on the sexual mores of society, and leaves everything exactly where it was before? Can we assert that the tendency to permit more and more to be shown and written about is a consequence, rather than a cause, of the general relaxation of moral rules? I think the evidence shows fairly conclusively that this notion is not very realistic, and that pornographic writings and pictures do have a definite effect in shifting the average person's behaviour in the direction of greater permissiveness.

Adherents of the abolition of censorship would be well advised to base their case on the harmlessness of sexual behaviours which are not actually subject to criminal proceedings; if they argue in terms of lack of proof for the 'tendency to deprave and corrupt', as many have done in the past, then it is to be feared that their arguments receive very little support from experimental psychology. I am neither arguing for nor against proposed changes in the rules governing censorship of books, plays, films or pictures. My concern is merely to set down the known facts.

What kind of evidence is available to indicate that pornography has any effect on people's behaviour? One might take the line of the British critic Milton Shulman and point out that directors of television companies who argue that sex and violence on the screen have no effect on people also argue (though usually in another place) that advertisements showing certain types of cars, or drinks, or chocolates have a tremendous effect in making people use that type of car, or drink, or chocolate; why the difference? If television advertising is effective (and there is little doubt that it is), then why should television be less effective when it advertises lax morals, cruelty and violence, and permissive behaviour generally? The attitude of television company directors is disingenuous, dishonest and absurd; it is clearly presented only to make it possible for the television companies to continue to coin money with the least effort.

Mr. Christopher Chattaway, then Britain's Postmaster General, who was responsible to Parliament for the activities of television, has publicly stated that if he knew of any such evidence, he would feel obliged to take action; his position hardly excused his ignorance. But he and his American equivalents, who also have claimed to hear no evil, speak no evil and see no evil with respect to the effects of television and film obscenity, are not alone in ignorance. Consider a recent Report on The Obscenity Laws by the Working Party set up by a Conference Convened by the Chairman of the Arts Council of Great Britain (this is the full title of the publication). Does obscenity corrupt? they ask, and answer that 'verifiable fact is virtually non-existent'. They quote as their authority a Professor R. M. Jackson, who is the Downing Professor of the Laws of England in the University of Cambridge; he writes that 'the supposed depravity and corruption by obscene articles is a matter of conjecture. No hard evidence can be put forward'. What he calls 'hard evidence' is, in the nature of the case, unobtainable, but even in law there is such a thing as circumstantial evidence, and this is at times sufficient to hang a murderer. The working party go on to quote a number of people, none of them familiar with the literature of experimental psychology; all acknowledge their ignorance, and no doubt others will now quote the ignorance of the working party as proof for the non-existence of evidence, and so the merry game continues.

We must, however, follow a scientific line of inquiry; and in science only the views of recognised scientists are considered, and a declaration that no evidence exists in a given field is only accepted from persons intimately concerned with that field. Such an attitude of scepticism might have helped the working party to arrive at a more sensible conclusion.

What kind of information would we regard as relevant to our question of whether pornography affects behaviour? We cannot take 10,000 virgins, expose half of them to television, or to pornographic books, while keeping the others way from any such infectious material, and then follow them up over a period of twenty years to find out which group produced more illegitimate babies – or whatever we might choose to be our criterion of 'conduct unbecoming a gentlewoman'. The answer must be in terms of the much more useful, indirect type of proof, just as, if we want to measure the speed with which remote stars recede from our galaxy, we must have recourse to the indirect measurement of the Doppler effect. In physics, indirect tests, in which deductions are made from theories, and then tested in the laboratory, far outweigh direct tests.

In behaviour therapy, particularly that part of it usually referred to as desensitisation therapy, a person suffering from a strong anxiety or fear reaction to a particular object or situation (snakes, or confronting a superior) is considered to have acquired a conditioned emotional reaction to the object or situation in question. The essence of desensitisation is the building up of conditioned approach responses to the objects or situations which produce fear; this is done by getting the subject to relax very deeply (or administering relaxing drugs), and then presenting him with minimally disturbing images of the objects or situations he fears. The disorders so treated are commonly referred to as neuroses, but this only means that they are 'maladaptive'; in England, a fear of snakes is absurd, and hence neurotic, but in Australia it might be useful, and save a person's life. Sexual anxieties and fears may be considered neurotic by the free-and-easy extravert, and morally and ethically advantageous by the introvert; there is no absolute scale on which we can measure social adaptivity. Consider now the lively effects of reading porno-graphic literature, or viewing sexually-arousing plays or films on television. The subject-matter produces a certain amount of anxiety (this has been experimentally verified in a number of studies made in the U.S.); however, viewing occurs under conditions which are the most relaxing, i.e. in the viewer's own home, sitting in his armchair, surrounded by his cherished possessions, etc. Hence conditions are arranged to promote maximal deconditioning (or desensitisation) of the fears and anxieties normally aroused.

As a consequence, the viewer or reader is able to tolerate even more outspoken material the next time, until finally he is in a position to go the whole hog and view (or read about) activities of a sexual nature which originally would have shocked him so much that he would have turned off the television, or thrown away his book.

What has been said here of sex is equally true and applicable when applied to violence. Our negative feelings when confronted with violence, the shedding of blood, and suffering are partly innate, partly acquired through a process of conditioning. They are essential for civilised society to survive; no police could cope with a population which was not constrained in their aggression by some form of conscience. But of course films, television viewing and modern books glorifying violence and aggression are in fact (if not by choice) breaking down this carefully built up set of conditioned responses. By showing these activities, which would normally be frightening and so aversive, in a slightly reduced form, and in the comfort of the reader's or viewer's own home, desensitisation must inevitably occur. If I were asked by some Martian invader how one could best destroy the human race without overt show of arms, I would have to say that the destruction of the moral and ethical standards which alone maintain a society would be the best method, and in order to achieve this aim I would have to say that the unrestrained and continued showing of violence on television and film screens throughout the country, day in and day out, was by far the easiest and cheapest way. People ask wonderingly why there has been such a terrible outbreak of violence in the U.S., where television programmes of this kind have been showing for much longer than anywhere else, and where saturation has been much more complete. I would answer that this is precisely what one would have predicted on psychological principles. But nobody asks psychologists about these things.

One of the most satisfactory methods of desensitisation is that of modelling, and it is here that we receive the strongest support for our thesis. Consider a person who is afraid of snakes, and cannot tolerate being in the same room with one. Sit him at a safe distance, then bring in a snake in your arms, showing no fear, and start to fondle the snake, curl it around your neck, and generally demonstrate that there is nothing to be feared. Gradually you will be able to bring the snake nearer, until finally the patient's fear is completely overcome, and he will start to fondle the snake himself. Many fears and anxieties have been overcome in this way, and the modelling can even be done symbolically, i.e. the snake handling can be done on film which is shown to the patient.

In the same way violence can be induced by film modelling. Children may be tested in situations where conflict arises over the possession of some toys; show a film, involving one child hitting the other, taking the toy and getting away with it, to some of the children, and another film, in which the child is punished for doing this, to the rest. Then put the children back into the same sort of sitution; what will they do? The answer, of course, is that they will imitate the modelled behaviour. Those who saw the film where the child got away with it will now be much more aggressive than before, while those who saw the film where the child was punished will now be less aggressive. There seems no doubt that films showing certain types of behaviours have a very strong influence on what children and adults do; imitation, to use this outdated term, is clearly a very powerful factor.

Some of the research done by the President's Commission may seem at first sight, to contradict these views. As the report puts it, 'there are two elementary, but fundamental, questions about erotic materials upon which nearly all concerns with the subject are based. First, does exposure to erotic stimuli sexually excite and arouse the viewer? Secondly, does such exposure affect the subsequent sexual behaviour of the user?' The first question is of course much easier to answer.

Sexual arousal can be measured along two quite different lines. We can ask our subjects to view (or read) pornographic material, and then ask them to rate the degree of their arousal on a 10-point scale. Or we can actually attach electrodes and other devices to their persons and measure the amount of physiological arousal. Results given by the first method leave little doubt about the arousing nature of pornographic material; between 60% and 85% of both male and female subjects in the Commission's tests experienced varying degrees of sexual arousal when presented with visual or printed material containing explicit reference to sexual behaviour. Males more often reported arousal from visual stimulation than from reading; females showed the opposite tendency. Females also reported 'disgust' more frequently than males. 'Blue films' are more potent than are stills in visual stimulation. These results are borne out by psycho-physiological studies, though these are rather complex and difficult to summarise.

Measurement of physical reactions can be direct or indirect. Direct measures can be taken, e.g. from the penis. Attach a strain gauge to it, or a simple plethysmograph (a device for measuring changes in volume), and you get a direct measure of the degree of erection consequent on exposure to the stimulus. This technique can be adapted to female subjects, but only with difficulty; one can measure, after a fashion, the increase in lubricity of what Masters and Johnson call the 'vaginal barrel', or one can measure the slight increase in temperature which accompanies sexual excitement in the same area, or one can measure the slight change in colour as the vagina becomes suffused with blood. Several such studies have left no doubt about the effectiveness of pornographic material, for both sexes. Another direct measure which has sometimes been used is the excretion of urinary acid phosphatase; this has been found to be greater after stimulation by erotic films than after stimulation by other erotic media.

Indirect measures are of a more general nature, e.g. heart rate, sweating or breathing; these have been found rather less suitable on the whole, particularly because they are so undifferentiated. You may react emotionally because you are disgusted, or annoyed, with the presentation, rather than because you are sexually aroused; indirect measures will not be able to differentiate these different reactions. Ideally one would seek for verbal report, direct measures, and indirect measures also, in assessing the effects of erotic stimulation; however, it is possible to overload the subject with electrodes, plethysmographs, and other bits of apparatus, to the extent that he cannot attend to the erotic stimuli themselves!

Sexual arousal depends to some extent on the sex of the viewer, and on the scenes viewed; males are more aroused than females by scenes depicting oral sex, for instance, while coitus produces equal degrees of arousal. (Generally oral sex appears to be more appealing to men than women.) Sexual experience is relevant; more physiological reactions are reported by experienced than by inexperienced subjects. One finding which anyone with experience in art could have predicted, but which is woefully disregarded by makers of 'blue' films, is that leaving something to the imagination is apparently more arousing then explicit presentations. In one study, subjects who were asked to think about some sexual themes without visual cues were twice as highly aroused as comparable subjects provided with literary stimuli. In another, subjects reported higher levels of arousal to films which had deleted a rape sequence, but implied its occurrence, as compared with films containing the scene. The same point is brought out by the fact that many subjects describe their reactions to explicit depiction of coitus scenes as 'boredom'; there is too little variety to maintain interest.

There appears to be a connection between the amount of pornographic material viewed or read by a person, and his general amount of sexual activity; the more active he is, the more pornography he consumes. This may appear unexpected; one might have thought that pornography would be an alternative to more normal sexual outlets, but the figures suggest otherwise. Early experience of masturbation seems linked with the other two variables; early masturbators tend to use pornography, and also seek early and frequent sexual contacts with the other sex. This is less surprising when one considers my own findings linking personality with sexual behaviour and attitudes; from these one might deduce that, on the whole personality determines the whole 'life pattern' of a person, and that viewing pornography would not produce much of a change in this pattern. This seems to be the conclusion come to by the various authors who studied this question, whose results are summarised in the President's report. 'These studies show that established patterns of premarital, marital and extramarital coitus, petting, homosexual activity, and sexual fantasy are very stable and are not substantially altered by exposure to sexually explicit stimuli'.

How are such conclusions arrived at? The typical experiment establishes a base-line, e.g. by asking participants to keep a detailed diary in which they record all sexual activities (coitus, masturbation, etc.). They are then exposed to the film(s) constituting the experimental stimulus, usually a very explicit 'blue' film depicting intercourse, oral sex, and/or some kind of perversion. Having viewed the film, subjects carry on keeping their diary, and entries preceding and following the films are compared. There are several such studies, both American and European, and the findings are remarkably similar; very little change, though a temporary increase may occur. The notion of the pure innocent viewing a pornographic film and immediately rushing out to rape the nearest virgin could hardly be more wrong.

What happens when normal subjects are given free access to all sorts of erotic material? The answer seems to be that satiation sets in quite quickly; subjects spend less time viewing 'blue' films, looking at pornographic pictures, and generally amusing themselves along these lines. At the same time, their physiological and psychological level of arousal in response to such material drops. This is a laboratory replication of events in Denmark after legalising pornography, when sales fell off, rather than increasing, as had been expected by many. 'Nine weeks after the daily exposure sessions ended, all subjects reported boredom and a number refused private opportunities to view erotica'. Thus, over-exposure tends to lead to loss of interest in pornography. There is, however, a recovery after several months; loss of interest is not permanent. Probably most subjects would settle down to a low level of exposure if they had their own way.

Inevitably, the Commission's report mentions in detail the results of the 'Danish experiment'. The 1969 repeal of the obscenity statute, allowing all forms of sexually explicit material to be sold, had been expected to be disastrous in many circles. In practice there was a marked decrease in reported sex crimes, the total falling from 783 (in 1966) to 591, 515 and 358 in subsequent years (in 1967 erotic literature became unrestricted). These are substantial decreases, amount to over 30% in 1969 alone; such a decline would be welcome in the U.S. and the U.K., where nothing comparable has happened. All classes of sex crimes decreased, but some decreased more than others. Rape and attempted rape decreased less than did exhibitionism or 'unlawful interference short of rape' with children, and these latter offences decreased less than voyeurism and homosexual offences, which showed the most dramatic decreases.

> Changes in the incidence of sex offences could not be attributed to legislative change, alteration of law enforcement practices or modified police reporting and data collection procedures. A survey of Copenhagen residents found that neither public attitudes about sex crimes nor willingness to report such crimes had changed sufficiently to account for the substantial decrease in sex offences between 1959 and 1969.

(The decrease preceded the abolition of the statute; during these years there had been a continual liberalisation of attitude by the law enforcement agencies.)

A more direct study of any possible relationship between sex crimes and pornographic material has recently been completed; this is not contained in the material surveyed by the Commission. In this study, rapists and child molesters were questioned in detail about their experiences with pornographic material; they were compared with non-criminal groups of similar social class, education and colour. (The study was made in the U.S., and it is important to compare white with white, black with black.) The results were quite clear-cut: 'Adolescent exposure to erotica was significantly less for all deviant and offender groups compared to the nondeviants. During adulthood, the sex offenders . . . continued to report less exposure to erotic stimuli than controls'. In addition it was found that 'less than a quarter of the respondents in any group imitated sexual behaviour seen in the erotic material immediately or shortly after its viewing. The hypothesis that extent of exposure during adolescence to erotica is positively associated with the later emergence of sexual pathology is not borne out by this study'. Such results may go counter to expectation, but they are not to be disregarded for that reason. In conjunction with the Danish experience, they make the conclusion almost mandatory that pornography does not by or of itself have a causal influence on the major sex crimes, such as rape, sex molestation of children, etc.

Other studies have shown that, if anything, sex offenders respond less strongly to pornographic material. One writer concluded from his study that

> about all that can be said is that strong response to pornography is associated with imaginativeness, ability to project, and sensitivity, all of which generally increase as education increases, and with youthfulness, and that these qualities account for the differences we have found between sex offenders, in general, and nonsex offenders. Since the majority of sex offenders are not well educated nor particularly youthful, their responsiveness to pornography is correspondingly less and cannot be a consequential factor in their sex offences unless one is prepared to argue that the inability to respond to erotica in general precludes gaining some vicarious stimulation and satisfaction and thereby causes the individual to behave overtly which, in turn, renders him more liable to arrest and conviction.

In fact, clinical studies of the early family history of sex offenders even suggest that they tend to come from repressive homes where sexual matters are not discussed openly, where there is a low tolerance of nudity, and punitive or indifferent parental responses to children's sexual curiosity and interest. As children, these future offenders encounter less in the way of erotica than does the average child, and this tendency apparently continues into adolescence – pictures of coitus are seen by the average child at fourteen, by the future offender at eighteen! As the report says: 'Such literature . . . suggests that sex offenders' inexperience with erotic material is a reflection of their more generally deprived sexual environment. The relative absence of such experience probably constitutes another indicator of atypical and inadequate sexual socialisation'.

We can now see why the abolition of pornographic censorship in Denmark may indeed have caused a lowering of the sex crime rate; if sex crimes are in part due to too puritanical an upbringing, then greater social permissiveness may indeed have a prophylactic effect on the youngsters involved. Looked at from this point of view, one might conclude that pornography plays an important educational role, a role which neither parents nor teachers at the moment are filling adequately.

The majority report of the Commission thus presented a very strong case in support of its main legal recommendation, namely that 'the Commission recommends that federal, state and local legislation should not seek to interfere with the right of adults who wish to do so to read, obtain, or view explicit sexual materials'. But it should be borne in mind that the commissioners were concerned to 'make a case', and that in doing so they may not always have been entirely scrupulous about weighing the evidence impartially.

This is the main charge of the critics, spelled out in detail by Dr. Victor Cline, a well-known psychologist from the University of Utah. He maintains that

a careful review and study of the Commission majority report, their conclusions and recommendations, and the empirical research studies on which they were based, reveal a great number of serious flaws, omissions and grave shortcomings which make parts of the report suspect and to some extent lacking in credibility. Readers of the majority report are at the 'mercy' of the writers of that report, and must assume that evidence is being presented fairly and in good faith on both sides of the issue . . . A number of the research studies upon which the report is based suggest significant statistical relationships between pornography, sexual deviancy and promiscuity. Yet, some vital data suggesting this linkage are omitted or 'concealed'. Findings from seriously flawed research studies or findings which do not follow from the data are sometimes presented as fact without mentioning their very serious limitations.

Note here one example of the kind of omission Cline refers to. This is a study by Davis and Braucht into the relationship between exposure to pornography and moral character. They found 'exposure to pornography, is the strongest predictor of sexual deviance among the "early age of exposure" subjects. In general, exposure to pornography in the "early age of exposure" subgroup was related to a variety of precocious heterosexual and deviant sexual behaviours.' They note that since exposure in this subgroup was not related to having deviant peers (bad associations and companions), it would be difficult to blame the sexual promiscuity and deviancy of these subjects on other factors. This research was contracted and financed by the Commission, and is mentioned many times in the report – but 'not a single mention is made of these negative findings'.

Cline's main point might be said to be this. The researches reported have shown that relatively short exposures to pornographic material of students and non-student adults have minimal effects on their sexual behaviour and their sexual attitudes. This is interesting, but of limited value. These are all fairly experienced individuals, usually of good education, and mentally non-pathological; the crucial question is what exposure to these materials would do to youngsters of poor education, and with slightly pathological mental make-up. In short, the experiments answer some questions, but they do not answer precisely those questions which are of most concern.

What short exposure to pornographic material does to well-integrated adults is one thing; what long-term exposure to such materials may do to not-so-well integrated youngsters is quite another. The writers of the majority report do not enter the necessary caveats in discussing these researches; they tend to generalise too freely, from one group to other groups dissimilar in age and character, and from short, often single exposures, to lengthy and multiple exposures. Such generalisations are not permissible, and though one may recognise the ethical difficulties involved in presenting such material to children, say, or of going beyond the limits of single or at most very limited presentations, nevertheless these limitations should be recognised and emphasised. Failure to do so implies a slide from scientific discussion to propaganda.

Worse, the majority report suppresses information that goes against its recommendations. One example has been given; Cline gives many more. It might be argued that all the information is in fact contained in the ten volumes of detailed research findings published separately from the report, but this is no real defence. Few people would rush out to buy and read these highly technical monographs after having waded through the report's 700 jargon-packed pages.

I think that there is no doubt that in part at least Cline is right. The evidence presented is interesting and important, but it does not justify the majority's opinions. If I were asked to state the conclusion to be drawn from the evidence I would say that any conclusions must be very tentative, but that certain points do emerge. Whether these justify any social action, rather than suggesting the need for further research, I will leave to the reader.

There seem to be important differences between individuals in their degree of sexual libido, general sexual motivation, or 'randiness' if you like. Some people, generally extraverted in personality, have a much more active sex life than others, generally introverted in personality. They engage in petting earlier, have intercourse earlier, have intercourse with more different partners, in more different positions, indulge in 'perversions' and deviant practices more actively, and generally behave in a manner one might designate 'libertine' or 'permissive'. Such people also tend to read and view pornographic material early in life, and the crucial question is one of causation: does the strong libido of the extravert make him look at pornography at an early age? Or is it the exposure to pornography that makes him show all the varied traits of the 'libertine'? Cline would presumably choose the second alternative; the majority-report writers the first. It must be admitted that there is no hard-and-fast evidence on which to base a decision – and this was admitted by the majority-report writers, though perhaps not as prominently as might be desired.

My own work would seem to suggest that pornography appeals to, and is sought out by those who have inherited extraverted proclivities, and who would in any case have a more active sex life, i.e. by the more extraverted type of person. As far as the evidence goes, and circumstantial as it is, it does support, if only mildly, this general conclusion.

Besides the extraverts who enjoy pornography and also lead a very 'sexy' life, there is a group of sex-starved people who also consume a great deal of pornography. These are people who score highly on the 'neuroticism' scale of the personality inventory I used – not pathological neurotics such as we find in mental hospital outpatient departments, but people who are 'tending that way'. They often have difficulties in their sexual lives – *ejaculatio praecox,* failure to achieve orgasm, frigidity, impotence – as well as mental symptoms, like mood swings, headaches, etc. For them, one might think, pornography is an alternative outlet for their sexual desires (which are very strong). Afraid to contact people of the other sex, they have recourse to erotic material which is pornographic or obscene. Again there is no direct evidence, but the indirect evidence (e.g. from studies of twins) suggests fairly strongly that neurotic disabilities, however mild, are likely to have a genetic background, and that the anxiety/fear responses to members of the opposite sex, and the turning to pornography instead, are due to these genetic factors – and possibly to early childhood experiences not themselves involving pornography.

These are reasonable suppositions, but of course social action requires much stronger evidence. I feel that in the nature of things it will always be extremely difficult, if not impossible, to rig up authentic experimental replicas of the sort of everyday encounters with pornography that anti-pornography exponents really object to. Inevitably, the experimenter can only expose his subjects to a limited short-term set of pornographic materials; what may be doing the damage, in the opinion of many, may be the general penetration of pornographic material into every corner of our culture.

More important than the furtive sale of obscene material in the Times Square or Soho bookstore may be the blatant exposure of female thighs in miniskirts going up the subway stairs, the bra advert on the posters, and the nude in the tabloid. It may be this constant insistence on sexual stimulation, even in quite irrelevant contexts, which produces a climate of opinion in which 'obscene' pornography plays only a minor part, but which tends to 'deprave and corrupt' many of those who come into contact with it. This climate of opinion may be the crucial variable, with published hardcore pornography only the tip of the iceberg, which leads to general permissiveness, increases in illegitimate pregnancies, abortions and venereal disease.

Again it would be difficult to establish which is the cause and which the effect; quite likely all these different factors are interacting in complex ways. Even if this 'general climate' view is correct, it is difficult to see what could be done about it – assuming that we would wish to do something about it. Short of banning bra adverts, forcing all women to wear maxis, and eliminating pictures of bare breasts from the press, we can hardly reverse the permissive trend. Certainly the banning of really obscene material could play only a minor part in changing the climate of opinion.

It is here, I think, that battle is really joined – do we want to reverse present trends, or do we welcome them? Do we prefer an extraverted or an introverted society? Do we prefer libertinism or puritanism? Such large-scale opinion studies as have been done suggest that we want neither of these extremes; the vast majority prefer something in-between – as indeed fits the majority of people's personalities, which are intermediate between extreme extraversion and extreme introversion. In other words, most people look for compromises; they tend to be easier to live with than extremes. Writers, philosophers and other moulders of public opinion tend to be carried to extremes by their eloquence; hence the view that people are embattled along rigid lines of pro and con. Nothing of the sort; most people firmly hold to the middle ground. The majority report tried to break away from this middle ground, and President Nixon firmly slapped it into place. It is doubtful if it could have been more successful had its argumentation been less one-sided.

So far our arguments have dealt entirely with reasonably normal people, but among sex criminals, the evidence is a good deal more clear-cut. It does seem that a greater freedom to publish obscene material may help the potential sex criminal to suppress or sublimate his libidinal impulses. Again, the evidence is not conclusive; but I doubt if many experts would dispute that sex crime is not increased by the open sale of explicit sexual material, and may very well be curtailed. This is an important conclusion, and should certainly be borne in mind when making decisions in this complex field.

One further argument is advanced by those who disagree with the conclusions of the President's Commission. They argue that obscenity escalates – that public showing of intercourse, oral sex, and various perversions soon makes these lose their 'spice', and that even more decadent forms of titillation will be put up for sale. This has happened in Denmark, where torture scenes, intercourse with animals, and scenes involving small children are now openly for sale. Even the most determined opponent of censorship may balk at this escalation and ask in particular whether those taking part in the actual filming (e.g. the children) should not receive some protection. As some connection between sex and cruelty has often been suggested by psychiatrists, this may be a very sensitive area in which to allow unfettered commercialism.

After all these pros and cons can anyone really be much wiser? Surely some firm conclusions should be possible? I can only say that, the evidence being what it is, to draw firm conclusions is to go quite outside the field of science. We must admit that at the moment we do not know anything like as much as we would like to know; research is urgently needed in many areas. Censorship is bad for some; obscenity is bad for some. We are faced with an ineluctable choice between two evils; clearly there is no easy way out.

Perhaps the final solution will be found in a distinction between voluntary and involuntary participation. You choose to view a pornographic film, read an obscene book, look at erotic pictures; you are much less free to choose a T.V. show, control what you come across in the newspaper, or encounter in the advertisements on the train. Of course one can switch off T.V. but by then the impression has already been made. Many people find nudity, or explicit sexual behaviour, offensive when encountered in this manner; nor may they be pleased to find nude students cavorting in the sunshine outside their universities. To call this 'prudery' is an uncalled-for value judgment; one man's meat is another man's poison. Nor is there any call to label such people 'repressed' or 'neurotic'; psychiatric concepts are too frequently used as terms of abuse, regardless of evidence. In any case, this is a two-sided weapon; as we have seen, many neurotics have recourse to pornography precisely because of their neurotic difficulties. Society has to pay attention to all its members, and if a large number do not wish to have their homes invaded by what they consider pornography, this puts T.V. and the other media mentioned into quite a different category from 'blue' films or 'dirty' pictures, which a person would only encounter if he actively sought them out.

Perhaps an acceptable compromise might be arrived at on this basis: greater freedom for the type of pornography which has to be sought out and is normally hidden, less freedom for the type of pornography which a person cannot avoid easily. This is the same kind of compromise which Britain's Wolfenden Committee recommended in the case of prostitution; they knew that they could not abolish prostitution, but they could and did remove it from the streets where it was likely to cause offence to many people. Compromises like this are always a little ridiculous, but they may cause the minimum of damage to society; this is their great virtue.

One last point should be made. Underlying all the discussions about pornography, obscenity, and our present perilous moral conditions, is the assumption that we now live in a 'swinging' society, with premarital sex, adultery, and all sorts of vices and perversions everywhere. This assumption is assiduously fostered by the mass media, but I have found little evidence for its accuracy in my own studies. There was much evidence for girls preserving their virginity until they met 'Mr. Right' (or thought they had), for great interest in personal relationships, and against 'sleeping around'. Similar conclusions emerge from the most recent study of *Sex and Marriage in England Today* by Geoffrey Gorer; he too found little evidence for the assumed prevalence of 'easy sex' and casual love-making. Exaggeration of current trends appears to be just as prevalent in the U.S., where figures similar to Gorer's are available. What Gorer discovered was that the 'great majority of the younger married men and women still put a very high value on marital fidelity', that 'a quarter of our male respondents and one tenth of our female respondents is the largest group to whom the journalistic phrase "permissive" can possibly be applied with any accuracy', and that 'despite the impression given by contemporary mass-communications with all the emphasis of the "permissive society", "swinging London", and the like in reporting, and the prevalence of erotic themes in much fiction (not to mention the disappearance of the taboo on printing a few common-speech words) England still appears to be a very chaste society, according to the replies of our informants.' These 'informants' constituted a random sample of the population; of this random sample, 'a quarter of our married male informants and nearly two-thirds of our married women said they were virgin at marriage; and a further 20% of the men and 25% of the women married the person with whom they first had intercourse'. Taking these groups together, Gorer argues that 'it would appear that just under half the men (46%) and nearly nine-tenths of the women (88%) reached the stage of marriage as technical virgins'.

Figures like these put a rather different complexion on the state of modern morality. As I pointed out in connection with my own findings, 'when all is said and done, more is said than done'. There is certainly less hesitation in talking about sexual themes, and even using the occasional four-lettered expletive in circumstances where this would have been unthinkable twenty years ago, but talking and doing are two different things. All the fine talk about liberation from ancient taboos has not led to the anticipated consequences; as Gorer makes clear, the song about 'love and marriage' still attracts the overwhelming majority of young people. Impersonal sex is probably no more widespread than it was when I was a student; the difference is simply that people talk about it more, and that the arts and the media in general are freer to exploit sexual themes and issues. Youngsters who grow up expecting the life of Reilly when they become teenagers, or go to university, may have a rude shock!

Even this not altogether large swing to permissiveness is already leading to a swing back to less permissive and more orthodox behaviour. In the United States, which tends to be ahead of the U.K. by a few years in all these swings of the pendulum, there is a marked decline in such things as the membership of 'free sex clubs'; the executive director of the Sexual Freedom League has resigned; and according to reports the number of Americans experimenting with group sex has fallen by two thirds in two years. The notorious '101 Club' in Hollywood has closed down, as have many other similar ones; Heffner's *Playboy* empire is in disarray, and his bunny girls may soon have to fend for their lettuce elsewhere. Dr. G. Bartell, in his carefully-researched book on *Group Sex,* declares that he sees a clear-cut retreat from sexual frivolity. There is a resurgence of marriage; a greater percentage of youngsters are getting married than ever before, and so are divorced men (women are a little more careful in this respect). The laws about obscenity and pornography, which were being set aside by Supreme Court judgments, are again being enforced more widely. Clearly the era of permissiveness is giving way to a less permissive one.

These swings must be perplexing to those who still hold to the old-fashioned (and erroneous) view that sex (like hunger) is a primitive desire which demands satisfaction, and that anything we may do to prevent its expression simply produces repression and neurosis.

Modern research has provided a much needed corrective to the rather primitive views, held even a few years ago, of sex as a biological instinct, rather like hunger and thirst; its aim was orgasm, and everything preceding this was only a preliminary. This single-act philosophy, held strongly by the Freudians, is so over-simplified as to be completely misleading. A hen will tend to eat a certain portion of the grain given it; increase the total amount, and the hen will eat more *in toto*. Many animals will eat more when put with another animal which is also eating. Thus even the most clearly 'instinctive' activities, in very primitive animals, are subject to social influences; how much more so the sexual 'instinct' in higher animals! Harlow has shown that when monkeys are brought up in isolation they showed no desire for sexual activity when put in a cage with other monkeys. Sexual appetite is certainly in large part acquired. When Schofield studied the sexual behaviour of young adolescents he found that of those who had had sexual intercourse, most had not enjoyed it much – less than half of the boys, and less than a third of the girls had thought it much fun! Clearly social factors were paramount in producing and perpetuating a form of conduct which had little intrinsic satisfaction.

F. A. Beach, whose work on sex in man and animal is well known, has made this point very clearly: 'Sexual appetite . . . has little or no relation to biological or physiological needs'. The sexual appetite is 'a product of experience, actual or vicarious'. In one experiment a penis plethysmograph was used, i.e. an instrument to measure the volume of the penis, in order to measure sexual arousal. Slides of shoes were shown to male subjects; these produced no reaction. Then slides of nude women were shown; these produced strong reactions. Now the conditioning procedure was begun; slides of shoes preceded by a second or two slides of nude women. After a while, the slides of shoes produced penis arousal even when not followed by the unconditioned stimuli: what is more, the conditioned stimuli showed generalisation, in that slides showing boots and other types of footwear also produced sexual responses, although they had never been paired with the nude slides. D. H. Lawrence kept cursing 'sex in the head', by which he meant the socially conditioned determinants of sexual arousal; he was more concerned with orgasmic mechanisms. But if we abolished 'sex in the head' we would abolish nearly all sex.

If sex is a biological need pure and simple, rather like hunger and thirst, then it must be satisfied regardless of social and other consequences; to try and avoid such satisfaction is in fact impossible. On this view pornographic films and books do no harm; people have sexual instincts anyway, and no added fuel is provided by these films and books. The appetite theory leads to rather different conclusions. Modern society is extending ever farther the field of the sex-conditioned stimuli, thus creating more and more stimuli and conditions which are conducive to sexual arousal. Within our biological limits, we have as a society chosen to maximise sexual arousal; this may or may not be a wise choice, but let us not deceive ourselves about this matter. There is a choice, and this choice is not pre-empted by biological necessity. It may not be open to the individual to make such a choice; it may be made for him by those who are in command of the mass media, particularly television. But this makes it all the more important that the decision should be made in the full consciousness of what is involved; at the moment it goes by default – there is no informed argument, and hence rational decisions are impossible to arrive at.

Reading pornographic literature has the obvious effect of providing reinforcement, in the same way as reading a motoring magazine tends to concentrate the interest on the purchase of a new car! A pornographic book gives you information (sometimes true, often false, but the reader does not know this!) about the many ways in which intercourse can be undertaken, how sexual appetite can be aroused and satiated in different ways, and what sorts of consequences can be expected. Better sources of information can, of course, be imagined, but as long as these are not available – or if available do not carry with them the same amount of reinforcement as do pornographic novels – many people will continue to derive their knowledge of patterns of sexual behaviour and mores, and the appropriate emotional accompaniments of sex, from such novels.

The factual information provided (or believed to be provided) by pornographic literature can be very important; it is not often realised how misleading is the information on which many people have to rely in this field. I remember my first 'patient', whom I encountered when I was doing research as psychologist to the Mill Hill Emergency Hospital during the war. Our patients were neurotic or psychotic soldiers and airmen, and one of them told me that the main reason for his breakdown was his incapacity to have intercourse; he had tried many times, but never succeeded. It turned out that he had only tried it standing up! I pointed out to him that it might be easier lying down, and as he did not seem to know much about it I lent him a copy of *Fanny Hill*. He devoured it within a day or two, and on his day off I saw him racing off to the bus (he lived in London, fortunately). When he came back he was glowing with happiness, and told me all about his brilliant success. If only pornographic literature were more factual in its accounts, how useful it could be for the purpose of providing information alone! As it is, many men, finding that they are unable to achieve the countless bouts per night which the heroes of these books seem to find so easy, fall prey to ideas of unworthiness and inferiority.

Many other false beliefs are promulgated and endorsed by pornographic books, and the same is true of sex manuals. To quote Masters and Johnson, in their well-documented book on *Human Sexual Response,* which is based entirely on their own extensive experimental investigations:

> Most marriage manuals advocate the technique of finding the clitoris and remaining in direct manual contact with it during attempts to stimulate female sexual tensions. In direct manipulation of the clitoris there is a narrow margin between stimulation and irritation. If the unsuspecting male partner adheres strictly to marriage manual dictum, he is placed in a most disadvantageous position. He is attempting proficiency with a technique that most women reject during their own automanipulative experiences.

This rather waspish comment is followed by their own recommendation:

> As stated previously, no two women practice automanipulation in similar fashion. Rather than following any pre-conceived plan for stimulating his sexual partner, the male will be infinitely more effective if he encourages vocalisation on her part. The individual woman knows best the areas of her strongest sexual focus and the rapidity and intensity of manipulative technique that provides her with the greatest degree of sexual stimulation.

This is good sense. People differ, and it is a mistake to generalise too freely about patterns of sexual conduct.

Pornography clearly presents a problem; is there an answer? Probably not; the problem is not a factual one, nor a technological one. You might ask if pornography is a good or bad thing, a use or an abuse of the media employed to purvey it. But such questions only seem meaningful: they depend on the answer one gives to another question, namely: what do you mean by 'good' in this context? Pornography does not have one set of consequences, but many; some might be considered good, others bad. Furthermore, what is good for one person may be bad for another; individuality is supreme in this field. It would be very foolish indeed to come down on one side or the other and say with conviction that pornography is or is not an abomination which should be banned from television, the screen and the printed page.

Some arguments can be dismissed pretty well out of hand. We cannot agree with the abolitionists that pornography induces people to commit sex crimes; unlimited permission to publish and show pornographic material of any kind may not seriously lower the sex crime rate, but it does not seem to put it up. Nor does freedom to publish pornography turn society into pornographers; there is evidence from Denmark that when pornography is freely permitted to appear, then after a short period of increased interest sales drop disastrously, and the whole business is kept alive only by exports to other countries still maintaining the taboo on such productions. Both these arguments used to be advanced with some effect by the abolitionists; their disproof is pretty thorough.

On the other side, it cannot any longer be argued with any degree of conviction that pornography, or the portrayal of violence, have no effect on the behaviour of the people who see these things on the screen, or read about them in books and magazines. Laboratory evidence shows quite clearly that effects of even quite short pieces of film modelling certain types of behaviour have a pronounced effect on the actual behaviour of children and adults; so do verbal representations. Both behaviour and emotional reactions are affected, and the effects are not transitory. The evidence is admittedly indirect, but that is not really a valid point of criticism; much scientific evidence in the 'hard' sciences is of this kind, and is readily accepted on much the same level as direct evidence. Thus, those who would wish to abolish censorship cannot reasonably go on arguing that pornography should be permitted because it has no effect on behaviour or emotion. This argument never carried much weight, being seen to be unreasonable and counter to experience with other types of 'advertising' – and much pornographic writing, from Walter to D. H. Lawrence, and from Henry Miller to Frank Harris, is similar in intent to advertising; these writers want desperately to convince the reader that their outlook on sexual matters is right and the orthodox outlook wrong.

The argument thus shifts to different ground, one where it should have been conducted from the beginning, free from all the red herrings which so many protagonists have dragged across the path. What the argument is about is simply the nature of the society in which we wish to live, and in which we wish our children to live – neither more nor less. We tend to think of people as being introverted or extraverted, but clearly we can extend this typology to societies. Puritan society was introverted; opposed to smoking and drinking, wenching and dancing, intent on moral and religious questions, on serious behaviour and deep thought. The permissive society is extraverted; fond of materialistic belongings, sensually appearing trappings, music, dancing, smoking and drinking, with an emphasis on sexual pleasure and no thought for the morrow. Advertising has taken the place of the Bible, pornography that of the Lives of the Saints, burlesque that of the religious meeting.

As Plato saw all too clearly, societies propagate their value system through the writings they encourage or tolerate, the poems they produce and publish, the pictures they paint, or the films shown in their cinemas. Societies engage in a gigantic process of brainwashing in order to ensure some degree of conformity; a process which makes use of the principles of conditioning. The little American boy who is made to salute his flag at school every morning and pledge allegiance to his country, is being brainwashed as surely as the Russian boy who is made to read about the divine intervention of Lenin in the power-struggle after the first war, or the Chinese boy who is made to carry Mao's Thoughts around in his satchel. Brainwashing is an inevitable part of welding together a society out of recalcitrant, individualistic pieces.

If we want to live in a society which stresses permanent, secure and loving union between a man and a woman, then pornography (and all the other forces which it stands for in this connection) certainly provide a threat, and a serious one at that. What does the advocate of permissiveness have to say? He would point out that all too often the alleged values of traditional marriage are mere pretence; that children often suffer more in unhappy homes than they would if their parents were to separate and follow their own inclinations in sexual matters. He would go on to point to the repressions involved in the old system, the evils of prostitution which apparently cannot easily be separated from monogamous marriage, and he would protest on aesthetic grounds against any form of licence or inspection for works of art; the artist must be completely free to follow his genius, regardless of consequences. These arguments too are fine and incontrovertible; given the existing value system of the advocate, the permissive society is obviously preferable to puritanism. In fact, both sides simply show the favourable consequences of their policies to the public, and try to hide the less acceptable ones.

Victorian repressiveness almost certainly failed to have the desired effect of promoting happy family life, security of upbringing and permanence of emotional attachment; these are all difficult to legislate for. Our own society, by extending the boundaries of what is socially acceptable without destroying completely the legal and moral warp and woof that regulates the nature of more permanent unions is probably nearer a true compromise. It is always difficult to say when a compromise is working most efficiently, but in the absence of further information one has the uneasy feeling that any extension of permissiveness would not only reduce general happiness and contentment, but create a strong impetus for the pendulum to start swinging back towards repressiveness.

Let us make no mistake; genuine information on most of the issues raised here is almost entirely lacking. We know practically nothing about the proportion of happy and unhappy marriages, the influence on children of the actions parents may take when their marriage is breaking down, or the changes in the number of extramarital and premarital affairs. Research into sexual matters is still in its infancy, and while a little is known, much, much more remains to be explored. It is a tragedy that such research is almost shunned by experimenters, grant-giving bodies and universities alike; the intrepid investigator is looked down on as a dirty old man whose thoughts are preoccupied with pornography. When I wrote to heads of colleges and other learned institutions to ask permission to approach their students in connection with the sexual questionnaire discussed earlier, many seemed offended at being asked, refused permission curtly and sometimes offensively, and some wrote long letters beseeching me to consider the error of my ways and return to the bosom of the mother church. Others pointed out the uselessness of research in this area, implying that they knew all there was to be known about these things – or at least, all that was worth knowing. These were all eminent literary or scientific men. Reactions from other sources were even more absurd. The head of a modelling agency wrote in high dudgeon to a variety of newspapers complaining that her girls were being exposed to unmentionable dangers.

What I think is needed is for the media to finance an independent research organisation, or at least give generous research grants to independent investigators, for research into the problems raised in this article. In Britain, the government makes it a statutory duty for the chemical industry to do research on drugs, and furnish the results to an independent government-appointed committee, for the simple reason that some of the products are dangerous, and the public needs protection. In exactly the same way I would suggest that some of the products of the mass media are dangerous, and that the public is entitled to protection.

It might be objected that our knowledge is so much greater in the psycho-pharmacological field, but this is simply not true. The panic measures taken when some pesticides, some oral birth control pills, and some sweeteners were banned did not originate in relevant, well controlled and properly executed research. The amount of knowledge in all these cases was minimal. Had nothing more substantial been available in the psychological field, I would certainly never have considered writing this article.

In the absence of such detailed knowledge, can we make any reasonable suggestions as to what society ought to do? Extremists on the one side demand complete freedom to exploit the sexual curiosity and the neurotic hang-ups of many people (mostly male) who wish to see explicit sexual scenes either on the stage or on the screen; extremists on the opposite side would like to use the law to make the screening of all such material illegal. Where on the continuum of sexual activity would they draw the line? Our sexual activities questionnaire, drew up a scale going from 0 (no sexual activity) to 15 (highest point on the scale), giving points intermediate between these extremes to each activity, according to the frequency with which each activity was reported. The result is shown in Table 3. What should be banned? Anything above 5 points? Even to raise such a question is to indicate the great difficulty of all censorship in this field. I have drawn up a formula for measuring the degree of obscenity in a given book (in my *Psychology is about People*), and the same could be done for films or stage plays by an adaptation of the data in Table 3. Any such cut-off point would of course be an uneasy compromise, and open to ridicule; should we even consider legal action in this field?

The main reasons given by adherents of censorship are quite clear. They are offended by the widely publicised advertisements for such films; they wish to protect their children from being seduced by such displays of permissiveness; they wish to protect marriage against the strains which open display of sexual activity might put upon it; they wish to protect women (and now even children) who might be forced to act in such films by threats of having their careers ended if they refuse to co-operate. They fear the effects of such films on the attitudes of those who see them; most such films treat women as sex objects and advocate male chauvinism. Such films play down love,

Table 3

Scale of Sexual Activity	Points
1. Social talking	0
2. One minute continuous lip kissing	3
3. Manual manipulation of female breast, over clothes	4.5
4. Manual manipulation of female breast, under clothes	5.3
5. Kissing nipples of female breast	6.3
6. Manual manipulation of female genitals	6.5
7. Manual manipulation of male genitals	7.2
8. Mutual manual manipulation of genitals	7.3
9. Sexual intercourse, face to face	8.3
10. Manual manipulation of male genitals to ejaculation	8.6
11. Oral manipulation of female genitals	10.3
12. Oral manipulation of male genitals	10.8
13. Sexual intercourse, man behind woman	12.2
14. Mutual oral-genital manipulation	12.5
15. Oral manipulation of male genitals to ejaculation	12.8
16. Mutual oral manipulation of genitals to mutual orgasm	15.0

tenderness, and all the human emotions which render our love-making different from that of animals, and those who favour censorship see this as a threat to civilised living. They see such films as advertisements for a permissive society in which they do not wish to live, and in which they do not wish to bring up their children. They urge that they have not only the right, but even the duty, to protect society against what they usually designate 'filth'. These are not unreasonable objections to obscene and pornographic material.

Those who are opposed to censorship often invoke freedom of expression, and the need to protect artistic integrity. These are not very strong arguments. Freedom is inevitably curtailed in all societies; we do not tolerate a person's freedom to incite to racial violence, for instance, and there are many other fields in which, for the sake of a higher good, we give up some of our liberties. If a good case be made out that the public showing of nudity and sexual intercourse on the stage or screen was essential to an artist's intention, then one might reconsider this point. No such case has in fact been made out. It is well known that art that leaves something to the imagination is more powerful than full-scale realism; the desire to 'show everything' is probably pure commercialism parading in the guise of artistic integrity. Indeed, nudity and explicit sexual conduct are very likely to inferfere with the artistic message of the film or play, because they arouse strong irrelevant feelings and emotions which distract the viewer from the main point of the play.

The strongest argument of the group opposed to all censorship is of course the statement: 'I am an adult, and I do not see why someone else should tell me what I am allowed to see or not to see'. This argument, too, has a number of answers. It may be all right for you to see this film, but would it be all right for a youngster to see it? Or a very unstable person? You can claim that by giving the film an 'X' Certificate you can keep out the youngsters, but we all know that this is mere pretence. At an impressionable age, and without any knowledge of the world to protect him, the message of the film may have a powerful influence on the youngster which might lead him along lines that in retrospect he might feel were not in his best interests. Even an adult who voluntarily goes to see an obscene film may find that the contents are upsetting, and have long-term effects that he may not like. And many people who go 'voluntarily' may do so only because they want to fall in with suggestions emanating from some peer group, or some powerful individual whom they wish to pacify. 'Consent' has many meanings and facets which might have to be analysed before we can readily say that 'consenting adults' means simply that people are doing something of their own free will, without unspoken constraints and motivations.

I have here laid more stress on the arguments in favour of censorship (with or without a legal basis) than on those against, because those against are probably better known than those in favour. This should not be interpreted as saying that personally I favour one side or the other. I am perhaps the only person who is not certain that he knows the right answer to this intractable problem; indeed, I am certain only of one thing, namely that there is no single, clear-cut answer to the problem at all. Society as a whole must decide what it wants, and society clearly is not of one mind in this respect, but contains many divergent sub-groups, each holding different views. There must be better ways of finding out what society wants than the clumsy device of having juries of 'twelve good men and true' pronouncing on the obscenity or otherwise of a film, play or book.

If there are to be any laws restricting the publication of 'obscene' matter, it is clear that the criterion of 'obscenity' will have to be changed drastically. Recent jury decisions have demonstrated that the man in the street is utterly confused by the meaning of phrases like 'tending to deprave or corrupt', and is unable to reach conclusions in a field where experts are clearly in disagreement. The law would need to apply a purely factual yardstick, such as that of verbal obscenity, which I suggested in *Psychology is about People,* or a visual one deriving from the facts listed in Table 3. The law would then simply say that anything printed that exceeded a stated number of points of Eysenck's formula was *eo ipso* obscene, or that any act shown on films or in the theatre scoring above 5.5 points on the scale of sexual activity was forbidden to be shown. T.V. could adopt a voluntary restriction not to go beyond a point somewhat lower on the same scale. Of course these suggestions would raise many problems, but nothing like as many as those raised by the present laws which are too subjective to be workable.

Social psychological research can perhaps tell us with somewhat greater accuracy what 'the man (and the woman) in the street think'. But whatever the outcome, there almost certainly must come about a compromise between the extremes; neither side is likely to be an outright winner. Or if one side should win (as the permissive side at one time seemed to have won in some of the states of the U.S.A.), then there will soon arise a backlash which will more than restore the balance. No preaching, however impassioned, is likely to win over adherents of the opposite side, and I doubt if factual evidence is likely to prove much more efficacious with many people. They feel strongly about these issues, and act in conformity with the 'law of certainty' I mentioned at the beginning of this article. If only we could leave the battlements, and arrive at some meaningful, sensible compromise, how much happier everybody might be in the long run!

REFERENCES

Bandura, A. *Aggression: A Social Learning Analysis.* Englewood Cliffs, New Jersey: Prentice Hall (1973).

Bandura, A., Ross, D. and Ross, S. A. 'Vicarious reinforcement and initiative learning'. *J. Abn. Soc. Psychol.,* (1963), **67**, 601–7.

Beach, F. A. *Hormones and Behavior.* New York: Harper & Bros. (1948).

Cline, V. B. *Where do you draw the Line? An exploration into media violence, pornography and censorship.* Provo, Utah: Brigham Young University Press (1974).

Eysenck, H. J. *Psychology is about people.* London: Allen Lane (1973).

Eysenck, H. J. *Sex and Personality.* London: Open Books (1976).

Eysenck, H. J. *You and Neurosis.* London: Maurice Temple Smith (1977).

Ford, C. S. and Beach, F. A. *Patterns of sexual behaviour.* London: Eyre & Spottiswoode (1952).

Goldstein, M. J., Kent, H. S. and Hartman, J. J. *Pornography and Sexual Deviance.* Berkeley: University of California Press (1974).

Gorer, G. *Sex and Marriage in England Today: A study of the view and experience of the under 45s.* London: Nelson (1971).

Masters, W. H. and Johnson, V. E. *Human Sexual Response.* Boston: Little, Brown (1966).

Rachman, S. and Hodgson, R. J. 'Experimentally induced "sexual fetishism" replication and development.' *Psychol. Record,* (1968), **18,** 25–7.

Thouless, R. H. 'The tendency to certainty in religious beliefs.' *Brit. J. Psychol.,* (1935), **26,** 16–31.

U.S. Commission on Obscenity and Pornography. *The Report of the Commission on Obscenity and Pornography.* New York: Bantam Books (1970).

LIST OF CASES

INDEX